INSTRUCTOR'S MANUAL

to accompany

THE LONGMAN WRITER

Rhetoric, Reader, Research Guide, and Handbook
Eighth Edition

THE LONGMAN WRITER

Brief Edition
Rhetoric, Reader, and Research Guide
Eighth Edition

THE LONGMAN WRITER

Concise Edition
Rhetoric and Reader
Eighth Edition

Judith Nadell

John Langan
Atlantic Cape Community College

Eliza A. Comodromos

Longman

Boston   Columbus   Indianapolis   New York   San Francisco   Upper Saddle River

Amsterdam   Cape Town   Dubai   London   Madrid   Milan   Munich   Paris   Montreal   Toronto

Delhi   Mexico City   São Paulo   Sydney   Hong Kong   Seoul   Singapore   Taipei   Tokyo

Instructor's Manual to accompany Nadell/Langan/Comodromos, *The Longman Writer: Rhetoric, Reader, Research Guide, and Handbook,* Eighth Edition; *The Longman Writer, Brief Edition: Rhetoric Reader, and Research Guide,* Eighth Edition; *The Longman Writer, Concise Edition: Rhetoric and Reader,* Eighth Edition.

Copyright © 2011, 2009, 2006, and 2003, Pearson Education, Inc.
All rights reserved. Printed in the United States of America. Instructors may reproduce portions of this book for classroom use only. All other reproductions are strictly prohibited without prior permission of the publisher, except in the case of brief quotations embodied in critical articles and reviews.

1 2 3 4 5 6 7 8 9 10–OPM–13 12 11 10

Longman is an
imprint of

www.pearsonhighered.com

ISBN-10: 0-205-01878-5
ISBN-13: 978-0-205-01878-9

CONTENTS

Part 4: The Research Paper
[Full and Brief versions only; **does not appear in Concise Edition**]

Part 6: A Concise Handbook
[Full version only; **does not appear in Brief Edition or Concise Edition**]

THEMATIC
CONTENTS

Ethics and Morality

Family and Children

Humor and Satire

Meaning in Life

Memories and Autobiography

Gender and Race

Nature and Science

Media and Technology

Instructor Resource Center

GETTING REGISTERED

To register for the Instructor Resource Center, go to **www.pearsonhighered.com** and click **"Educators."**

1. Click **"Download teaching resources for your text"** in the blue welcome box.

2. Request access to download digital supplements by clicking the **"Request Access"** link.

Follow the provided instructions. Once you have been verified as a valid Pearson instructor, an instructor code will be e-mailed to you. Please use this code to set up your Pearson log-in name and password. After you have set up your user name and password, proceed to the directions below.

DOWNLOADING RESOURCES

1. Go to http://www.pearsonhighered.com/educator and use the "Search our catalog" option to find your text. You may search by Author, Title, or ISBN.

2. **Select your text** from the provided results.

Longman Writer, The: Rhetoric, Reader, Research Guide, and Handbook, 8/e
Nadell, Langan & Comodromos
©2011 | Longman | Paper; 688 pp | Not Yet Published
ISBN-10: 020579839X | ISBN-13: 9780205798391

3. After being directed to the catalog page for your text, click the **Instructor Resources** link located under the **Resources** tab.

Clicking the Instructor Resources link will provide a list of all of the book-specific print and digital resources for your text below the main title. Items available for download will have a 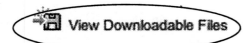 icon.

4. **Click on the View Downloadable Files** link next to the resource you want to download.

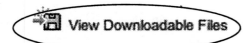

A pop-up box will appear showing which files you have selected to download. Once you select the files, you will be prompted to log in with an Instructor Resource Center log-in.

5. Enter your log-in name and password, and click the **"Submit"** button.

6. Read the terms and conditions and then click the **"I accept"** button to begin the download process.

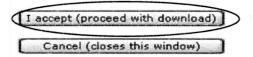

7. **"Save"** the supplement file to a folder you can easily find again.

Once you are signed into the IRC, you may continue to download additional resources from our online catalog.

Please "Sign Out" when you are finished.

What Is MyCompLab™?

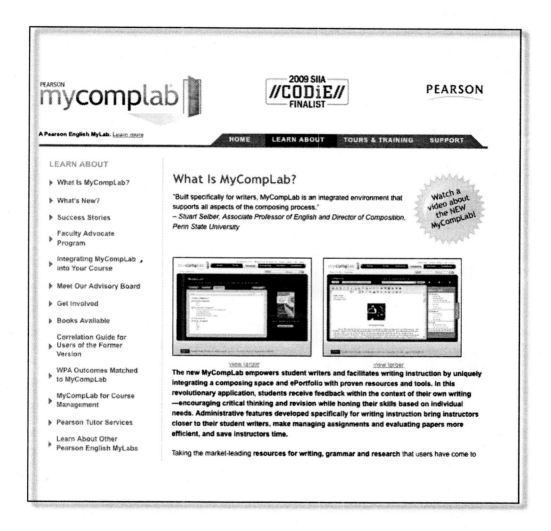

How Do Students Register?

It is easy to get started! Simply follow these easy steps to get into your MyCompLab™ course.

1 **Find Your Access Code** (It is either packaged with your textbook, or you purchased it separately.) You will need this access code and your CLASS ID to log into your MyCompLab™ course. Your instructor has your CLASS ID number, so make sure you have that before logging in.

2 Click on "Students" under "First-Time Users." Here you will be prompted to enter your access code, enter your e-mail address, and choose your own Log-In Name and Password. **Once you register, you can click on "Returning Users" and use your new log-in name and password every time you go back into your course in MyCompLab™.**

xvi

More on Registering

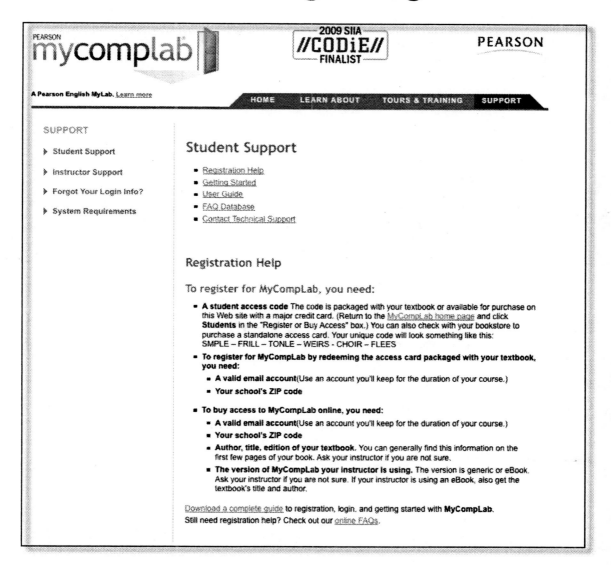

SUPPORT

- Student Support
- Instructor Support
- Forgot Your Login Info?
- System Requirements

Student Support

- Registration Help
- Getting Started
- User Guide
- FAQ Database
- Contact Technical Support

Registration Help

To register for MyCompLab, you need:

- **A student access code** The code is packaged with your textbook or available for purchase on this Web site with a major credit card. (Return to the MyCompLab home page and click **Students** in the "Register or Buy Access" box.) You can also check with your bookstore to purchase a standalone access card. Your unique code will look something like this: SMPLE – FRILL – TONLE – WEIRS - CHOIR – FLEES
- **To register for MyCompLab by redeeming the access card packaged with your textbook, you need:**
  - **A valid email account**(Use an account you'll keep for the duration of your course.)
  - **Your school's ZIP code**
- **To buy access to MyCompLab online, you need:**
  - **A valid email account**(Use an account you'll keep for the duration of your course.)
  - **Your school's ZIP code**
  - **Author, title, edition of your textbook.** You can generally find this information on the first few pages of your book. Ask your instructor if you are not sure.
  - **The version of MyCompLab your instructor is using.** The version is generic or eBook. Ask your instructor if you are not sure. If your instructor is using an eBook, also get the textbook's title and author.

Download a complete guide to registration, login, and getting started with **MyCompLab**.
Still need registration help? Check out our online FAQs.

Resources

MyCompLab™ provides Resources topics in writing, grammar, and research. These Resources are available to all users of MyCompLab™, whether you are working on your own or in an instructor's course.

Each topic includes instructional, multimedia, and/or exercise resources.

- **Instructional resources** define concepts and provide examples of the concept. For some instructional resources, a QuickCheck appears at the end of an instruction. A QuickCheck is one or two questions or examples, and you select the correct answer or example. MyCompLab™ then displays a pop-up identifying whether your answer is correct or incorrect and why.

  For eBook courses, the instructional resource list also has a link to the relevant section in the eBook.

- **Multimedia resources**, when available, are typically audio clips or videos that reinforce a concept. The multimedia resources include animated and narrated tutorials that range from grammar topics, strategies for developing a draft, guidelines on peer reviews, and tutorials on avoiding plagiarism to deciding on the topic for a paper.

- **Exercises** provide you with the opportunity to practice and apply what you have learned. MyCompLab™ provides immediate feedback to your answers, letting you know whether your answer is correct or incorrect, which answer is correct, and why that answer is correct. MyCompLab™ also provides refresher resources to further reinforce the concept. The results of these exercises are logged in your Gradebook's Practice Results.

  Most topics have multiple sets of exercises to provide extensive practice. However, once you complete all the exercises for a topic, MyCompLab™ displays a **Take Again** link so you have the option of reworking a topic's exercises. The score you get when you retake the exercises replaces the original score.

TIP: A topic's exercises can be recommended by MyCompLab™ based on the results of a diagnostic assignment or by your instructor when commenting on your writing submissions.

MyCompLab™ organizes instruction, multimedia, and exercise content by topic. However, you also have access to a Media Index that organizes the content by type (for example, all videos in one list).

TEACHING COMPOSITION WITH
THE LONGMAN WRITER

Teaching offers many pleasures. Among the foremost, for us, is the chance to get together with colleagues for some shoptalk. Trading ideas, airing classroom problems, sharing light moments, speculating about why some assignments set off fireworks and others fizzle—all of this helps us in our day-to-day teaching.

In this *Instructor's Manual*, we would like to share with you some thoughts about teaching freshman composition and about using *The Longman Writer*. We'll explain our approach for introducing each pattern of development and indicate what we emphasize when discussing the professional essays in each section. We'll provide suggested answers to the activities that conclude each of the writing-process chapters and to the prewriting and revising activities that follow the introductions to the patterns of development. We'll also offer suggested answers to the "Questions for Close Reading" and "Questions About the Writer's Craft" found after each professional essay. These responses aren't meant to be definitive. Although we purposely avoided open-ended, anything-goes questions, we intend the responses to represent *our* views only. You may not agree with all our interpretations. That's fine. If nothing else, our answers may suggest another way of viewing an essay.

AT THE START OF THE COURSE

Frankly, many students dread freshman composition—a bitter pill to swallow for those of us who have made the teaching of writing our lives' work. But it's important to understand that many students' past experiences with writing have not been positive. Rather than trying to pretend that all our students are pleased about being in a writing class, we work to get out in the open any unhappiness they may have about writing and writing teachers.

Here's how we go about airing any negative feelings that may exist. On the first day of class, we acknowledge students' feelings by saying something like, "I guess some of you wish that you didn't have to take this course. In fact, you may feel that the only thing worse would be having to take a course in public speaking." Our remark elicits smiles of self-recognition from many students, and the whole class seems to relax a bit. Then we

Copyright © 2011, 2009, 2006, 2003 by Pearson Education, Inc.

ask students to talk about why they have such uneasy feelings about taking a writing course. Many have sad tales to tell about previous writing classes and writing teachers. Here are summaries of some of the comments we've heard over the years:

- In the past, my papers were returned so covered with red ink that I could barely make out my own writing. I felt discouraged to see how much I had done wrong and angry to see my work covered over with comments.

- I could never figure out what my teachers wanted. Different teachers seemed to look for different things. Since there were no clear standards, I've never understood the qualities that make up good writing.

- Writing papers always took me too much time and felt like an endless chore. Getting a first draft done was hard enough, but revising was even worse. And the payoff for writing several drafts didn't seem worth the effort.

- I knew in my head what I wanted to say but didn't know how to get my thoughts down on paper. My ideas never came out quite right.

- I had writer's block whenever I sat down to put pen to paper. I started at the desk, daydreamed, fidgeted, and had real trouble getting started. Finally, just before an assignment was due, I dashed off something to hand in, just to get it over with.

As such sentiments are aired, students discover that their experience has not been unique; they learn that others in class have had similar frustrating experiences. In addition, we tell the class that each semester many of our students recount comparable sagas of woe. We reassure the class that we understand the obstacles, both inner and outer, that they have to face when writing. And we tell them that we will work to make the freshman writing course as positive an experience as possible. But we also say that we'd be dishonest if we told them that writing is easy. It isn't. And, unfortunately, we have no magic formula for turning them into A-plus writers. On the other hand, because we are writers and because we work with writers, we know that the composing processes can be satisfying and rewarding. We tell the class that we hope they'll come to share our feelings as the semester progresses.

From here, we move to an activity that continues the ice breaking while also familiarizing the class with the workshop format we use frequently during the semester. Students form groups of two and then four, chatting with each other for about five minutes each time. To get them moving, we put some questions on the board: what are their names, where are they from, where are they living while attending college, what other courses are they taking, what is their intended major, and so on. After a few seconds of nervous silence, the class begins to buzz with friendly energy.

When ten minutes or so have passed, we stop the activity and explain why we have devoted some precious class time to socializing. During the semester, we explain, the class will often meet in small groups and respond to each other's work, learning a good deal from each other about writing as they do so. So it makes sense for them to get to know each other a bit right at the outset. Also we explain our hope that they will find sharing their writing as interesting and enjoyable as chatting together. Then, as a final step in building a spirit of community, we create a class e-mail directory by circulating a piece of paper on which all the students have the option of writing their names and e-mail addresses. Before the next class, we have the sheet typed and reproduced so that everyone participating can have a copy.

ASSIGNING THE FIRST CHAPTERS IN THE BOOK

During the first or second class, we emphasize to students that the course should help them become sharper readers as well as stronger writers. With that in mind, we assign the chapter on "The Reading Process" before moving on to work on the writing process.

When students come to class having read the reading chapter, we answer any questions they may have and go over the "Questions for Close Reading" and "Questions About the Writer's Craft" that follow the selection from Ellen Goodman. (See pages 27–28 of this manual.)

After this discussion of reading, we begin introducing the writing process, explaining how helpful it is for a writer to break down the task of writing into stages. We've found that many students have never viewed writing as a process, and our explanation of the steps is a great revelation to them. We are careful to emphasize that not everyone writes the same way; we explain that after trying out our recommendations about each stage of the process, students will most likely vary the process in a way that works best for them. We then assign the first part of Chapter 2, "Getting Started Through Prewriting" (up to "Discovering Your Essay's Limited Subject," p. 22). In the next class, we discuss and practice prewriting. We tell the class that prewriting loosens a writer up. Exploratory and tentative, prewriting helps reduce the anxiety many people feel when facing the blank page. With prewriting, a writer doesn't have to worry, "This better be good." After all, no one except the writer is going to read the prewritten material. We work briefly with activities, such as Activities 1 and 3 at the end of Chapter 2, but we tell our students that the best way for them to discover what prewriting is like is for them to try it for themselves. Therefore, we say, "Let's suppose you had to write an essay on why students dislike English classes or what teachers could do to make English courses more

3

interesting." Then we ask them to select one prewriting technique discussed in the book (questioning the subject, brainstorming, freewriting, or mapping) to generate the raw material for such an essay. Often we distribute scratch paper or yellow lined paper for them to use, reinforcing the message that prewriting is tentative and vastly different from finished work. Instructors who ask students to keep a journal might instead have them write a first journal entry in class.

At the end of the class, we ask students to save the prewriting just prepared in class for possible use as the basis for an essay later in the term. And we assign the rest of the prewriting chapter and an additional end-of-chapter activity; we also ask them to begin keeping a journal.

In the next class, we finish the discussion of prewriting and work again in class on getting familiar with the various prewriting techniques. After this, we introduce the patterns of development as invaluable aids to the writing process, from prompting ideas to organizing them coherently to easing the flow during the writing of a draft. For the next class, we assign either Chapter 10, "Description," or Chapter 11, "Narration," as the first in-depth study of a pattern of development. We have found both patterns invaluable in helping beginning writers attend to detail, discover appropriate sequencing, and become aware of the reader's needs. Throughout the course, we alternate in-depth study of the stages of the writing process with work on the patterns of development. And we frequently have students reach back to material generated in the early prewriting sessions and, after feedback from other students, use it as the basis for more polished work.

WAYS TO USE THE BOOK

The Longman Writer is organized into six sections; most writing courses will emphasize Part Two, the nine chapters on the writing process, and Part Three, covering the nine patterns of development: description, narration, illustration, division-classification, process analysis, comparison-contrast, cause-effect, definition, and argumentation-persuasion. The study of the writing process can be handled in at least two ways. You might wish to spread in-depth work on each of the writing-process steps through the semester, while also assigning professional selections and discussing some of the patterns of development. Or you may wish to devote the first unit of the course to work on the writing process before moving into the selections and the patterns of development. In Part Three, the introduction to each pattern shows how the writing process applies to the pattern; the more accessible experiential patterns are presented first, before moving on to the more demanding analytic patterns.

If you organize your course according to the patterns of development, you need not feel confined by the order of patterns in the book; each chapter is self-contained, making it possible for you to sequence the modes however you wish. And, of course, there's no need to cover all the essays in a chapter or even all the patterns. You may wish to concentrate on one or two of the selections demonstrating a pattern rather than attempt to cover them all in depth. A word of warning: If you tell the class which of several assigned selections will be emphasized, some students will read only those. You'll probably want to explain to students that there are many ways to use a pattern and that reading *all* the assigned essays will give them an understanding of the options available.

For courses organized according to the patterns, we suggest that you emphasize early in the semester that professional writers don't set out to write an essay organized in a particular way. Rather the patterns emerge as writers prewrite and organize their ideas; writers come to see that their points can best be made by using a particular pattern of development or combination of patterns.

It's helpful, we've learned, to assign selections before *and after* students write an essay. For example, if students are going to write a causal analysis, you might have them read "Why We Crave Horror Movies" and "Black Men and Public Space." Then, after reviewing their drafts and seeing the problems they have had, for example, with a chain of causes and effects, you might have them examine the way Kleiner handles the interplay of causes and effects in "When Mañana Is Too Soon."

Some instructors using the patterns-of-development approach in their courses place a special emphasis on exposition. If this is your orientation, you might want to focus early on the illustration chapter. That chapter stresses the importance of establishing a point. Then you might move to the description and narration chapters; these underscore the importance of, respectively, a dominant impression and a narrative point, both developed through specific supporting details.

If you prefer to design the course around themes rather than development patterns, the thematic table of contents (at the front of the textbook) will help you select essays on timely issues. For such a course, we recommend that you have students read a number of essays on a given theme. The fact that several essays on the same theme use different patterns of development helps students see that the patterns are not ends in themselves but techniques that writers use to make their points.

CREATING A PROCESS-ORIENTED CLASS ENVIRONMENT

We've found that creating a workshop atmosphere in the classroom helps students view writing as a process. When a new paper is assigned, we try to give students several minutes to start their prewriting in class. In other classes, time may be set aside for students to rework parts of their first draft. We may, for instance, ask them to sharpen their introductions, conclusions, sentence structure, or transitions.

In our experience, it's been especially productive to use class time for peer review of first drafts. For these feedback sessions, students may be paired with one other classmate, or they may meet with three or four other classmates. (We've found groups of more than five unwieldy.) Feedback from someone other than the course instructor motivates students to put in more time on a draft. Otherwise some of them will skip the revision stage altogether; as soon as they've got a draft down on paper, they'll want to hand it in. Hearing from other classmates that a point is not clear or that a paragraph is weakly developed encourages students to see that revision involves more than mechanical tinkering. They start to understand that revision often requires wholesale rethinking and reworking of parts of the essay. And after a few peer-review sessions, students begin to identify for themselves the problem areas in their writing.

You'll find that many students squirm at the thought of reacting to their classmates' work. So it's not surprising that they tend to respond to each other's papers with either indiscriminate praise or unhelpful neutrality. To guide students, we prepare a brief checklist of points to consider when responding to each other's work. You might, for example, adapt the checklists on pages 85–86, 87, 103–04, and 113–14 to fit a particular assignment. With such a checklist in front of them, students are able to focus their impressions and provide constructive feedback.

There are a number of ways to set up peer-review sessions. Here are a few you may want to use:

- After pairing students or placing them in small groups, have each essay read aloud by someone other than the author. Students tell us that hearing another person read what they've written is invaluable. Awkward or unclear passages in a paper become more obvious when someone who has never before seen the essay reads it aloud.

- Place students in small groups and ask them to circulate their papers so that everyone has a chance to read all the essays. Then have each group select one especially effective paper to read aloud to the rest of the class. Everyone discusses each paper's strengths and what might be done to sharpen the sections that miss the mark.

- Ask one or two students to photocopy their drafts of an assignment, making enough copies so that everyone can look at the papers. In class, the other students—either as a whole or in groups—react to the papers up for scrutiny that day.

A quick aside: At the start of the course, students are reluctant to "offer their papers up for sacrifice"—as one student put it. But once they're accustomed to the process, they are not at all skittish and even volunteer to be "put on the chopping block"—another student's words. They know that the feedback received will be invaluable when the time comes to revise.

6

As you can no doubt tell, we have a special liking for group work. Since it gives students the chance to see how others approach the same assignment, they come to appreciate the personal dimension of writing and develop an awareness of rhetorical options. The group process also multiplies the feedback students get for their work, letting them see that their instructor is just one among many readers. Group activities thus help students gain a clearer sense of purpose and audience. Finally, we have found that peer review encourages students to be more active in the classroom. When students assume some of the tasks traditionally associated with the instructor, the whole class becomes more animated.

SOME CAUTIONS ABOUT GROUP WORK

If you are new to group work, you may have the uneasy feeling that the group process can deteriorate into enjoyable but unproductive chat sessions. That *can* happen if the instructor does not guide the process carefully.

Here are several suggestions to steer you clear of some traps that can ensnare group activities. First, we recommend you give very clear instructions about how students are to proceed. Providing a checklist, for example, directs students to specific issues you want them to address. Second, we believe in establishing a clear time schedule for each group activity. We might say, "Take five minutes to read to yourself the paper written by the person on your left" or "Now that all the papers in your group have been read, you should vote to determine which is the strongest paper. Then take five minutes to identify one section of the essay that needs additional attention." Third, although we try to be as inconspicuous as possible during group work, we let students know that we are available for help when needed. Sometimes we circulate among the groups, listening to comments and asking a question or two. But, more often, we stay at the desk and encourage students to consult with us when they think our reaction would be helpful.

RESPONDING TO STUDENT WORK

Beyond the informal in-class consultations just described, we also meet during the course with each student for several one-on-one conferences of about 15 to 30 minutes. Depending on our purpose, student needs, class size, and availability of time, a number of things may occur during the individual conferences. We may review a paper that has already been graded and commented on, highlighting the paper's strengths and underscoring what needs to be done to sharpen the essay. Or we may use the conference to return and discuss a recent essay that has or has not been graded. In the last few years, we have tended not to grade or write comments on papers we're going to review in conference. Instead we take informal notes about the papers and refer to them when meeting with students. We've found that this approach encourages students to interact with us more freely since their attention isn't riveted to the comments and grade already recorded on the paper. Finally, we end each conference by jotting down a brief list of what the student needs to concentrate on when revising or writing the next assignment. Students tell us this individualized checklist lets them know exactly what they should pay attention to in their work.

When students hand in the final draft of a paper, we ask them to include their individualized checklists. Having a checklist for each student enables us to focus on the elements that typically give the student trouble. And, candidly, having the checklist in front of us tames our not-so-noble impulse to pounce on every problem in an essay.

In our oral and written comments, we try to emphasize what's strong in the essay and limit discussion of problems to the most critical points. Like everyone else, students are apt to overlook what they've done well and latch onto things that haven't been so successful. If every error a student makes is singled out for criticism, the student—again, like everyone else—often feels overwhelmed and defeated. So unless a student is obviously lackadaisical and would profit from some hard-hitting teacherly rebukes, we try to make our comments as positive and encouraging as possible. And rather than filling the paper with reworked versions of, let's say, specific sentences and paragraphs, we make liberal use of such remarks as these: "Read these last three sentences aloud. Do you hear the awkwardness? How could you streamline these sentences?" or "Doesn't this paragraph contradict what you say at the beginning of the preceding paragraph? What could you do to eliminate the confusion?"

When responding to a paper, we often suggest that the student review or reread a professional essay, the introduction to a rhetorical pattern, or a specific chapter on the writing process. And we always end our comments with a brief list of points to be added to the student's personalized checklist.

USING PORTFOLIOS TO ASSESS STUDENT PROGRESS

You may wish to have your students present a portfolio of their work for grading at the conclusion of the course, instead of giving grades for each paper in succession. Using such a portfolio system alters somewhat the way you respond to individual student papers as they are submitted, because you assign no grades to them. The written and oral feedback on a paper is geared solely to making the essay a more effective piece of communication rather than to justifying a particular low or high grade. This forces all concerned—instructors and students—to stay focused on how to improve writing rather than on what might pull a paper down or what score a paper should get. If students balk at "floating free" of grades for the whole course, you might occasionally supply a tentative grade or give students grades on one or two essays so they get a feel for the standards. As the course progresses, however, the issue of what a strong paper is like should be resolved. The students will be reading the successful papers in the text, examining and commenting on the essays of other students, and hearing a plenitude of helpful comments about writing.

You should indicate clearly at the start of the course that students must complete each essay as well as all other practices, journal entries, and so forth that you assign but that the writing component of their final grade will be based upon a portfolio of polished work. Clearly establish the minimum number of essays to be included in a completed portfolio. Typically, a course might be represented by four final-draft essays, plus some late-in-the-term in-class writing. In addition, you may wish to examine the successive drafts for one of the revised papers. To receive a grade, each student meets with the instructor for a conference about the writing progress demonstrated in the portfolio. After a dialogue about the writing's strengths and areas needing improvement, the instructor and student agree on a grade.

Such a portfolio system has several advantages. It stresses to students that writing well is an ongoing process and encourages them to make subsequent revisions of their essays as they acquire new insights into writing. It forces them to take responsibility for their progress beyond the achievement they reach in the first submitted version of an essay. It instills the notion of a writing community, for once they have gotten beyond the initial series of structured feedback sessions that you have built into the course, students must initiate feedback from their peers and from the instructor on any revisions they do. Finally, such a system dramatizes the reality that writers write for other people and that reaching the audience, not jumping hurdles to get a grade, is the goal of writing.

AT THE END OF THE COURSE

Since our students keep all their papers in a folder, they have no trouble retrieving essays written weeks, or even months, earlier. So, near the end of the semester we ask students to select—for one more round of revision—three or four essays, with each paper illustrating a different rhetorical pattern. We use these reworked versions of the essays to assign a final grade to each student. If you structure your course around themes and issues, you'll probably want to require that each paper deal with a different theme.

An especially rewarding way to end the semester is to have the class publish a booklet of the best writing. Students revise and then submit two of their strongest papers to a class-elected editorial board. This board selects one essay from each student in the class, making an effort to choose essays that represent a mix of styles and rhetorical approaches. After a table of contents and a cover have been prepared, the essays are retyped (or computer files of each are consolidated), duplicated, and stapled into booklet form (or posted online on a course Website).

Students respond enthusiastically to this project. After all, who can resist the prospect of being published? And knowing that their writing is going public encourages students to revise in earnest. The booklets yield significant benefits for us, too. They help build a bank of student writing to use as examples in subsequent semesters. As a bonus, the booklets allow us to reconnect with the experiences, thoughts, and feelings of the students passing through our classes year after year. Such booklets have been an ongoing source of pleasure.

A SUGGESTED SYLLABUS

On the following pages we present a syllabus that will give you some further ideas on how to use *The Longman Writer*. Note that the syllabus assumes the course meets twice a week for an hour and a half per session over the course of fifteen weeks. The syllabus can, of course, be adjusted to fit a variety of course formats.

WEEK 1

Class 1

*   Provide an introduction to the course and handle necessary business matters.

*   Direct a "getting to know each other" activity. (See pages 2–3 of this manual.)

*   Have students prepare an in-class writing sample to get an initial sense of their writing needs.

*   Assignment—Ask students to read Chapter 1, "Becoming a Strong Reader."

Class 2

*   Discuss Chapter 1, "Becoming a Strong Reader," including the reading and craft questions following "Family Counterculture."

*   Return the in-class papers. Review common sentence skills and mechanical problems.

*   Introduce the writing process, with emphasis on prewriting.

*   Assignment—Have students read up to "Discover Your Essay's Limited Subject" (p. 22) in Chapter 2, "Getting Started Through Prewriting."

WEEK 2

Class 3

- Discuss and answer questions about the first part of Chapter 2, "Getting Started Through Prewriting."

- Have students do some practice prewriting or a practice journal entry; ask for a few volunteers to submit their writing to be read aloud anonymously.

- Have students, in groups or as a class, do Activities 1 and 3 at the end of Chapter 2. Discuss answers as a class.

- Assignments—Have students:

   a. Finish Chapter 2, "Getting Started Through Prewriting." Do Activity 1 at the end of Chapter 2.

   b. Begin keeping a journal. Number and length of entries to be specified by the instructor.

Class 4

- Discuss and answer questions about the second part of Chapter 2, "Getting Started Through Prewriting." Go over Activity 1 at the end of Chapter 2.

- Have students do in class Activity 5 at the end of the chapter. Discuss results as a class; have volunteers read their prewriting aloud or submit for anonymous reading. Or have students share their prewriting with each other in groups.

- Introduce the first pattern of development, Description (or Narration, as you choose).

- Assignment—Have students read Chapter 10, "Description," up to "Revision Strategies" (p. 132) or, alternatively, Chapter 11, "Narration," up to "Revision Strategies" (p. 170).

12

WEEK 3

Class 5

- Discuss descriptive or narrative writing and answer student questions.

- Have students do in class Activities 1 and 6 at the end of Chapter 10, "Description." Alternatively, have them do Activities 1 and 3 at the end of Chapter 11, "Narration." Discuss the results as a class, or have student groups share the results of Activity 6 if done individually.

- Assignments—Have students:

  a. Finish Chapter 10, "Description," or Chapter 11, "Narration." Complete Activity 2 or 3 at the end of Chapter 10 or Activity 2 or 5 at the end of Chapter 11.

  b. Read "The Storm This Time" by David Helvarg or another selection in Chapter 10. Alternatively, read "Shooting an Elephant" by George Orwell or another selection in Chapter 11. Prepare to discuss the reading and craft questions following the assigned selection.

Class 6

- Discuss the assigned selection.

- Finish discussion of Chapter 10, "Description," or Chapter 11, "Narration." Have students do Activities 5 and 6 at the end of Chapter 10 or Activities 4 or 6 at the end of Chapter 11. Arrange groups so students may share their revisions of Activity 6 in Chapter 10 or Activity 6 in Chapter 11.

- Have students do prewriting for one of the writing assignments at the end of he assigned description or narration selection or at the end of Chapter 10 or 11. Using groups, have students share their prewriting and get feedback.

- Assignments—Have students:

a. Read a second assigned selection from Chapter 10 or 11 and prepare to discuss the reading and craft questions following it.

b. Prepare a draft of the description or narration essay.

WEEK 4

Class 7

- Discuss the assigned selection.

- Initiate peer review on students' description or narrative essays. (See pages 6-8 of this manual.) Give students the option of handing in their papers now or revising them by the next class.

- Assignments—Have students:

a. Revise the description or narrative essay (optional).

b. Read Chapter 3, "Identifying a Thesis."

Class 8

- Pass back and discuss students' description or narrative essays; collect essays from students who chose to revise.

- Discuss and answer questions about Chapter 3, "Identifying a Thesis."

- Have students do Activities 1 and 4 at the end of Chapter 3. Discuss the results.

- Assignments—Have students:

a. Do Activities 2 or 5 at the end of Chapter 3, "Identifying a Thesis."

b. Read Chapter 12, "Illustration," up to "Revision Strategies" (p. 203).

WEEK 5

Class 9

- Discuss assigned Activities 2 or 5 at the end of Chapter 3, "Identifying a Thesis."

- Discuss and answer questions on Chapter 12, "Illustration."

- Have students do in class Activities 1 and 2 at the end of Chapter 12. Use groups or pairs to share responses to both activities. Read aloud responses to Activity 2.

- Assignments—Have students:

  a. Do Activity 4 at the end of Chapter 12, "Illustration."

  b. Read "Bombs Bursting in Air" by Beth Johnson or another selection in Chapter 12 and prepare to discuss the reading and craft questions following it.

  c. Read Chapter 4, "Supporting the Thesis With Evidence." Complete Activity 1 at the end of Chapter 4.

Class 10

- Have students share results of Activity 4 at the end of Chapter 12, "Illustration," either in groups or by reading aloud to the class. If there is not enough time for group work, collect student responses and review quickly at home, without marking.

- Discuss the assigned reading selection.

- Discuss and answer questions on Chapter 4, "Supporting the Thesis With Evidence," and on Activity 1.

- Have students do in class Activity 2 at the end of Chapter 4. Also arrange groups and have them do Activity 3 or 4. Discuss the results.

- Assignment—Have students finish Chapter 12, "Illustration," and do Activity 5 at the end of the chapter. Also do Activity 5 at the end of Chapter 4.

WEEK 6

Class 11

- Go over Activity 5 at the end of Chapter 4.

- Discuss and answer questions on the rest of Chapter 12, "Illustration." Discuss the results of Activity 5 in Chapter 12.

- Have students do Activity 6 or 7 at the end of Chapter 12; arrange groups so students may share their revisions.

- Have students do prewriting for one of the writing assignments at the end of the assigned selection or at the end of Chapter 12. Using groups, have students share their prewriting and get feedback.

- Assignments—Have students:

  a. Prepare a draft of the illustration essay.

  b. Read a second assigned selection from Chapter 12, "Illustration," and prepare to discuss the reading and craft questions at the end of the selection.

Class 12

- Initiate peer review on students' illustration essays. (See pages 6–8 of this manual.) Give students the option of handing in their papers now or revising them by the next class.

- Discuss the assigned reading selection.

- Introduce Chapter 5, "Organizing the Evidence."

- Assignments—Have students:

  a. Revise the illustration essay (optional).

  b. Read Chapter 5, "Organizing the Evidence."

WEEK 7

Class 13

- Pass back and discuss students' illustration essays; collect essays from students who chose to revise.

- Discuss and answer questions in Chapter 5, "Organizing the Evidence." Have students do Activities 1, 2, and 4 at end of Chapter 5.

- Assignments—Have students:

  a. Do Activity 5 at end of Chapter 5, "Organizing the Evidence."

  b. Read Chapter 13, "Division-Classification," up to "Revision Strategies" (p. 237) and do Activities 1 and 2 at the end of Chapter 13. Alternatively, read Chapter 14, "Process Analysis," up to "Revision Strategies" (p. 271) and do Activities 1 and 2 at the end of Chapter 14.

  c. Read "The Men We Carry in Our Minds" by Scott Russell Sanders or another selection in Chapter 13. Alternatively, read "Talking About Editing" by David Shipley or another selection in Chapter 14. Prepare to discuss the reading and craft questions at the end of the selection.

Class 14

- Discuss Activity 3 at the end of Chapter 5, "Organizing the Evidence."

- Discuss and answer questions about Chapter 13, "Division-Classification." Go over Activities 1 and 2 at the end of Chapter 13. Have students do in class Activities 3 and 4 at end of Chapter 13. Alternatively, discuss and answer questions about Chapter 14, "Process Analysis," and go over Activities 1 and 2 at the end of Chapter 14. Have students do in class Activities 3, 4, or 5 at the end of Chapter 14.

- Discuss the assigned reading selection.

- Assignments—Have students:

a. Finish Chapter 13, "Division-Classification," or Chapter 14, "Process Analysis."

b. Read "What Are Friends For?" by Marion Winik or another reading selection in Chapter 13. Alternatively, read "What Shamu Taught Me About a Happy Marriage" by Amy Sutherland in Chapter 14. Prepare to discuss the reading and craft questions at the end of the selection.

WEEK 8

Class 15

- Discuss the rest of Chapter 13, "Division-Classification," and have students do Activity 5 at the end of the chapter. Alternatively, discuss the rest of Chapter 14, "Process Analysis," and have students do Activity 6 at the end of Chapter 14. Use groups to share results.

- Discuss the assigned reading selection.

- Have students do prewriting for one of the writing assignments at the end of the assigned division-classification or process-analysis selection or at the end of Chapter 13 or 14. Using groups, have students share their prewriting and get feedback.

- Assignments—Have students:

  a. Prepare a draft of the division-classification or process-analysis essay.

  b. Read Chapter 6, "Writing the Paragraphs in the First Draft," up to "Write Other Paragraphs in the Essay's Body" (p. 66) and do Activity 1 at the end of Chapter 6.

Class 16

- Initiate peer review on students' division-classification or process-analysis essays. (See pages 6–8 of this manual.) Give students the option of handing in their papers now or revising them by the next class.

- Discuss and answer questions on Chapter 6, "Writing the Paragraphs in the First Draft." Go over Activity 1. Have students do in class Activity 2 or 3 at the end of the chapter.

- Assignments—Have students:

    a. Revise the division-classification or process-analysis essay (optional).

    b. Finish Chapter 6, "Writing the Paragraphs in the First Draft," and do Activity 2 or 3 at the end of the chapter if not assigned in class.

WEEK 9

Class 17

- Pass back and discuss students' division-classification or process-analysis essays; collect essays from students who chose to revise.

- Continue discussing Chapter 6, "Writing the Paragraphs in the First Draft," and Activities 2 and 3 at the end of the chapter. Have students do Activities 4 and 5 or 6 at the end of the chapter.

- Introduce Comparison-Contrast.

- Assignment—Have students:

    a. Read Chapter 15, "Comparison-Contrast," up to "Revision Strategies" (p. 305). Do Activity 2 at the end of the chapter.

    b. In Chapter 6, "Writing the Paragraphs in the First Draft," do Activity 9 at the end of the chapter.

Class 18

- Discuss and answer questions on Chapter 15, "Comparison-Contrast," and go over Activity 2 at the end of the chapter. Have students do in class Activity 1 and either 3 or 4 at the end of the chapter. Use groups to share responses to Activity 3 or 4.

- Go over Activity 9 at the end of Chapter 6, "Writing the Paragraphs in the First Draft."

- In class, read "Euromail or Amerimail" by Eric Weiner in Chapter 15. Discuss the selection as an example of "one-side-at-a-time" format.

- Assignments—Have students:

  a. Read an additional selection in Chapter 15, "Comparison-Contrast," and prepare to discuss the selection's use of the "point-by-point" format. Also prepare to discuss the reading and craft questions following the selection.

  b. Finish Chapter 15, "Comparison-Contrast," and do Activity 6 at the end of the chapter.

WEEK 10

Class 19

- Discuss the assigned selection.

- Discuss the rest of Chapter 15, "Comparison-Contrast," and go over Activity 6 at the end of the chapter, perhaps using groups to share revisions. Have students do in class Activity 5 at the end of the chapter.

- Have students do prewriting for one of the writing assignments at the end of the assigned comparison-contrast selections or at the end of Chapter 15. Using groups, have students share their prewriting and get feedback.

- Assignments—Have students:

  a. Prepare a draft of the comparison-contrast essay.

  b. Read Chapter 7, "Revising Overall Meaning, Structure, and Paragraph Development."

Class 20

- Initiate peer review on students' comparison-contrast essays. (See pages 6–8 of this manual.) Ask students to use the guidelines and checklists in Chapter 7 during the peer-review process. Require students to revise their essays by the next class.

- Discuss and answer questions on Chapter 7, "Revising Overall Meaning, Structure, and Paragraph Development." Have students do in class Activities 1 and 3 at the end of the chapter.

- Assignments—Have students:

    a. Revise the comparison-contrast essay, using the revision checklist.

    b. Bring in journal entries, previously written essays, or material generated for Activity 6 at the end of Chapter 6 for revision practice in class.

WEEK 11

Class 21

- Collect the comparison-contrast essays.

- Go over Activity 3 at the end of Chapter 7, "Revising for Overall Meaning, Structure, and Paragraph Development," or use groups to share revisions of journal entries or previous papers.

- Assignment—Have students read Chapter 8, "Revising Sentences and Words," up to "Make Sentences Emphatic" (p. 100).

Class 22

- Pass back and discuss the students' comparison-contrast essays.

- Discuss the first part of Chapter 8, "Revising Sentences and Words." Have students do Activities 1 and 2 at the end of the chapter.

- Introduce Cause-Effect.

- Assignments—Have students:

   a. Finish Chapter 8, "Revising Sentences and Words." Do Activity 12 at the end of the chapter.

   b. Read Chapter 16, "Cause-Effect," up to "Revision Strategies" (p. 339).

WEEK 12

Class 23

- Discuss and answer questions on the rest of Chapter 8, "Revising Sentences and Words." Go over Activity 12 at the end of the chapter. In class, have students do Activities 3 and 4 at the end of the chapter.

- Discuss and answer questions on Chapter 16, "Cause-Effect." In class, have students do Activities 1 and 2 at the end of the chapter.

- Assignments—Have students:

   a. Do Activity 5 at the end of Chapter 8.

   b. Finish Chapter 16, "Cause-Effect," and do Activities 3 and 5 at the end of the chapter.

Class 24

- Go over Activity 5 at the end of Chapter 8, "Revising Sentences and Words." Have students do in class Activity 6 at the end of the chapter and discuss results. Using groups, have students work on Activity 8 at the end of the chapter.

- Discuss and answer questions on the rest of Chapter 16, "Cause-Effect." Go over Activities 3 and 5 at the end of the chapter. Have students do in class Activity 4 at the end of the chapter.

- Assignments—Have students:

a. Do Activity 11 at the end of Chapter 8, "Revising Sentences and Words."

b. Read two selections in Chapter 16, one emphasizing causes, "Why We Crave Horror Movies" by Stephen King, and one emphasizing effects, "Black Men and Public Space" by Brent Staples. Prepare to discuss the reading and craft questions following the selections.

WEEK 13

Class 25

- Go over Activity 11 of Chapter 8, "Revising Sentences and Words." Have students do in class Activity 9 or 10 at the end of the chapter.

- Discuss the assigned selections in Chapter 16, "Cause-Effect."

- Have students do prewriting for one of the writing assignments at the end of the assigned cause-effect selections or at the end of Chapter 16. Using groups, have students share their prewriting and get feedback.

- Assignment—Have students prepare a draft of the cause-effect essay.

Class 26

- Initiate peer review on students' cause-effect essays. (See pages 6–8 of this manual.) Ask students to use the checklists during the peer-review session.

- Introduce Definition or Argumentation-Persuasion as you choose.

- Assignments—Have students:

a. Revise the cause-effect essay, using the checklist.

b. Read Chapter 17, "Definition," up to "Revision Strategies" (p. 369). Alternatively, read Chapter 18, "Argumentation-Persuasion," up to "Revision Strategies" (p. 417).

23

WEEK 14

Class 27

- Collect the cause-effect essays.

- Discuss and answer questions about Chapter 17, "Definition," and have students work in class on Activity 2 at the end of the chapter and share responses in groups. Also do Activity 1 at the end of the chapter. Alternatively, discuss Chapter 18, "Argumentation-Persuasion," and have students work in class on Activity 2 at the end of the chapter and share responses in groups. Also do Activities 1 and 3 at the end of Chapter 18.

- Ask students to read "Beyond the Pleasure Principle" by Ann Hulbert or another selection in Chapter 17. Alternatively, assign "Driving to the Funeral" by Anna Quindlen or another selection at the end of Chapter 18. Discuss the reading and craft questions following the selection.

  Assignments—Have students:

  a. Finish Chapter 17, "Definition," and do Activity 3 at the end of the chapter. Alternatively, finish Chapter 18, "Argumentation-Persuasion." Do Activity 4 at the end of the chapter.

  b. Read "Life as Type A" by James Gleick or another selection from Chapter 17. Alternatively, read "How the Schools Shortchange Boys" by Gerry Garibaldi and "A War Against Boys?" by Michael Kimmel at the end of Chapter 18. Prepare to discuss the reading and craft questions for the assigned selection(s).

  c. Read Chapter 9, "Editing and Proofreading."

Class 28

- Pass back and discuss students' cause-effect essays.

- Discuss and answer questions about the rest of Chapter 17, "Definition." Go over Activity 3 at the end of the chapter. Have students do in class Activity 4 at the end of the chapter. Alternatively, discuss the rest of Chapter 18, "Argumentation-

Persuasion." Go over Activity 4 at the end of Chapter 18. Have students do in class Activities 5 and 6 at the end of the chapter.

- Discuss the assigned reading selections.

- Have students do prewriting for one of the writing assignments at the end of the assigned definition or argumentation-persuasion selections or at the end of Chapter 17 or 18. Using groups, have students share their prewriting and use the checklists when providing feedback.

- Assignments—Have students:

    a. Prepare a draft of the definition or argumentation-persuasion essay.

    b. Do Activity 1 at the end of Chapter 9, "Editing and Proofreading."

WEEK 15

Class 29

- Go over Activity 1 at the end of Chapter 9, "Editing and Proofreading."

- Initiate peer review on students' definition or argumentation-persuasion essays.

- Have students work in class on Activity 5 at the end of Chapter 17, "Definition." Alternatively, have students work in class on Activities 5 and 6 at the end of Chapter 18, "Argumentation-Persuasion."

- Assignment—Have students revise the definition or argumentation-persuasion essay.

Class 30

- Pass back and discuss students' definition or argumentation-persuasion essays.

- Have students submit their folders of revised work.

- Conclude the course.

ANSWER KEY

ANSWERS FOR CHAPTER 1
"BECOMING A STRONG READER" (p. 1)

FAMILY COUNTERCULTURE

Ellen Goodman

Questions for Close Reading (p. 13)

1. According to Goodman, parenting today entails a constant struggle against what the popular marketplace presents as attractive to children. She asserts, "What the media delivers to children by the masses, you are expected to rebut one at a time" (paragraph 14). In the past, she tells us, parents raised their children "in accordance with the dominant cultural message" (2). But today they must "raise their children in opposition" (14) to it. Responsible parenting, Goodman feels, is now a matter of resistance, making child raising an increasingly difficult task.

2. Both the grocers' association and PR people "assembled under the umbrella marked 'parental responsibility'" (5) protested the ban. Goodman takes the PR people more seriously because she considers them a symptom of a dangerous phenomenon: the tendency to call for more parental responsibility precisely at the time the marketplace becomes more irresponsible. To Goodman, this demand for an unrealistic degree of parental accountability absolves the marketplace of its responsibility.

Questions About the Writer's Craft (p. 13)

1. In the first two paragraphs, Goodman uses the second-person point of view to establish the fact that she is aiming her essay at parents: "All *you* [italics added] need to join is a child" and "At some point between Lamaze and the PTA, it becomes clear that one of *your* [italics added] main jobs as a parent is to counter the culture." The specific parents Goodman addresses are those struggling to raise their children in

27

opposition to mainstream culture. Goodman's use of "we" and "our" (16) makes it clear that she allies herself with these beleaguered adults. She argues that it's unfair to think that parents should be considered successful only if they can counter the culture. Such a standard, she asserts, is impossible to attain, given the pervasive power of media messages.

2. In paragraph 16, Goodman repeats the word "it's" four times. Goodman may repeat this word to illustrate just how familiar readers are with the problem: It is no longer necessary to identify the problem by name; it is so much a part of their daily lives that they already know, perhaps too well, to what she is referring. This repetition also reflects the ongoing nature of the struggle, the short, clipped assertions summing up the problem succinctly.

ANSWERS FOR CHAPTER 2
"GETTING STARTED THROUGH PREWRITING" (p. 14)

Below we provide suggested responses to selected activities at the end of Chapter 2 (pp. 31–33). In some cases, other responses are possible.

1. **Set A**

   3   Abortion
   2   Controversial social issue
   5   Cutting state abortion funds
   4   Federal funding of abortions
   1   Social issues

   Set B

   4   Business majors
   3   Students' majors
   1   College students
   2   Kinds of students on campus
   5   Why students major in business

2. "Day care," "male and female relationships," and "international terrorism" are clearly too broad to be used as topics for a two- to five-page essay.

3. Here are some descriptions of possible purposes, tones, and points of view for the various topics and audiences.

Overcoming shyness

— for 10-year-olds
Purpose: to reassure them, help them feel safer
Tone: lively, optimistic
Point of view: ex-shy adult

— for teachers of 10-year-olds
Purpose: to help teachers encourage shy children
Tone: explanatory
Point of view: psychologist

— for young singles
Purpose: to show how easy talking to others can be
Tone: pep talk
Point of view: an extroverted young single

Telephone solicitations

— for people training for a job
Purpose: to motivate
Tone: upbeat
Point of view: high-powered successful phone salesperson

— for homeowners
Purpose: to advise how to handle
Tone: angry
Point of view: experienced homeowner

— for readers of a humor magazine
Purpose: to make fun of telephone sales pitches
Tone: mocking
Point of view: call recipient

Smoking

— for people who have quit
  Purpose: to reinforce their decision with benefits
  Tone: supportive and informative
  Point of view: medically informed quitter

— for smokers
  Purpose: to demolish their reasons for smoking
  Tone: sarcastic
  Point of view: a smoke hater

— for elementary-school children
  Purpose: to warn them of dangers
  Tone: serious
  Point of view: a concerned parent

5. Here are some possible patterns that might work with these topics and purposes:

   a. Topic: the failure of recycling efforts on campus
      Pattern: cause-effect

   b. Topic: the worst personality trait that someone can have
      Pattern: description or illustration

   c. Topic: the importance of being knowledgeable about national affairs
      Pattern: argumentation-persuasion

ANSWERS FOR CHAPTER 3
"IDENTIFYING A THESIS" (p. 34)

Below we provide suggested responses to selected activities at the end of Chapter 3 (pp. 39–40). In many cases, other responses are possible.

1. **Limited Subject:** Privacy and computerized records

TB   Computers raise significant questions for all of us.

FS   Computerized records keep track of consumer spending habits, credit records, travel patterns, and other personal information.

OK   Computerized records have turned our private lives into public property.

A   In this paper, the relationship between computerized records and the right to privacy will be discussed.

2. Here are some possible thesis statements for the topics:

a. Topic: the failure of recycling efforts on campus
    Thesis: Campus apathy about recycling results from poor planning by the campus housing department.

b. Topic: the worst personality trait that someone can have
    Thesis: Bossiness is an intolerable trait in a friend.

c. Topic: the importance of being knowledgeable about national affairs
    Thesis: Gaining awareness of current events is a significant part of becoming a responsible adult.

3. Below are possible thesis statements for each pair of general and limited subjects.

General Subject	Limited Subject	Possible Thesis
Psychology	The power struggles in a classroom	The classroom is often a battlefield, with destructive struggles for power going on between students and teacher.
Health	Doctors' attitudes towards patients	In hospitals, doctors often treat patients like robots rather than human beings.

| Work | Minimum-wage jobs for young people | The minimum wage is too low to inspire young people to work hard and advance themselves. |

4. Below is a possible thesis statement for one set of points.

    Possible thesis: If not closely monitored, experiments in genetic engineering could yield disastrous results.

ANSWERS FOR CHAPTER 4
"SUPPORTING THE THESIS WITH EVIDENCE" (p. 41)

Below we provide suggested responses to selected activities at the end of Chapter 4 (pp. 46–47). In many cases, other responses are possible.

1. **Thesis**: Colleges should put less emphasis on sports.

    OK   High-powered athletic programs encourage grade fixing.

    TG   Too much value is attached to college sports.

    OK   Competitive athletics can lead to extensive and expensive injuries.

    OK   Athletes can spend too much time on the field and not enough on their studies.

2. Below are possible supporting points for each of the thesis statements.

    Thesis: Rude behavior in movie theaters seems to be on the rise.

    — People feel free to chat loudly with their companions during films.

    — Some shout out humorous or vulgar comments about the characters and events on the screen.

32

— Others smoke and visit the popcorn stand without any concern for those they disturb.

Thesis: Recent television commercials portray men as incompetent creatures.

— College male washing colors and whites together, to horror of older woman in laundromat.

— Father caring for child but unable to cope with emergency.

— Men concerned only with taste of product, while wives are knowledgeable about healthfulness.

Thesis: The local library fails to meet the public's needs.

— The hours are limited and inconvenient.

— The part-time, inexperienced staff provides insufficient assistance.

— The collection is outdated and incomplete.

ANSWERS FOR CHAPTER 5
"ORGANIZING THE EVIDENCE" (p. 48)

Below we provide suggested responses to selected activities at the end of Chapter 5 (pp. 54–55). In many cases, other responses are possible.

1. **Thesis**: Our schools, now in crisis, could be improved in several ways.

   I. Schedules
     A. Longer school days
     B. Longer school year
  II. Teachers
     A. Teacher-certification requirements
     B. Merit pay for teachers
 III. Curriculum
     A. Better textbooks for classroom use
     B. More challenging course content

2. **Set A**

   Thesis: Traveling in a large city can be an unexpected education.

   Purpose 1: To explain, in a humorous way, the stages in learning to cope with the city's cab system.

   This purpose would clearly require a chronological approach to depict "the stages in learning to cope. . . ."

   Purpose 2: To describe, in a serious manner, the vastly different sections of the city as viewed from a cab.

   This purpose would require a spatial approach, moving from section to section.

   Set B

   Thesis: Supermarkets use sophisticated marketing techniques to prod consumers into buying more than they need.

   Purpose 1: To convince readers that positioning products in certain locations encourages impulse buying.

   This purpose would require a spatial approach, covering the locations in order.

   Purpose 2: To persuade readers not to patronize those chains using especially objectionable sales strategies.

   This purpose would require an emphatic approach.

4. **Thesis:** Friends of the opposite sex fall into one of several categories: the pal, the confidante, and the pest.

   Overall pattern of development: Division-classification

   — Frequently, an opposite-sex friend is simply a "pal."

   Pattern of development: Definition

   — Sometimes, though, a pal turns, step-by-step, into a confidante.

   Pattern of development: Process analysis

34

— If a confidante begins to have romantic thoughts, he or she may become a pest, thus disrupting the friendship.

Pattern of development: Cause-effect

ANSWERS FOR CHAPTER 6
"WRITING THE PARAGRAPHS IN THE FIRST DRAFT"
(p. 56)

Below we provide suggested responses to selected activities at the end of Chapter 6 (pp. 74–78). In many cases, other responses are possible.

1. a. The topic is the final sentence of the paragraph: "Clearly, being an expert doesn't guarantee a clear vision of the future."

    b. The first sentence of this paragraph is the topic sentence: "A small town in Massachusetts that badly needed extra space for grade school classes found it in an unlikely spot." The final sentence identifies this "unlikely spot" as a saloon.

    c. The topic sentence is the first sentence: "Many American companies have learned the hard way that they need to know the language of their foreign customers."

2. Below are possible revised versions of the paragraphs.

    a. Other students can make studying in the college library difficult. For one thing, some students spread out their books, coats, backpacks, and other paraphernalia so that they take up a whole library table, leaving no room for anyone else. Whispering and giggling with friends, chomping gum, even eating sandwiches, others indulge in thoughtless behavior that makes concentration impossible. Still others, tapping their feet, clicking their pens, shifting noisily every two minutes, disrupt the quiet. Worst of all, some students remove books and magazines from their assigned locations and don't return them. Some even tear out pages, making it impossible for another person to find needed material.

35

b.   Some people have dangerous driving habits. Acting as though no one else is on the road, they blithely drop into a lane without giving other motorists any warning. Others seem unsure of where they're going; they move around the road without signaling, hustling into the turn lane and then veering back to their original position. The truly confused, of which there seem to be many, conscientiously blink for a right turn and then turn left. Finally, some motorists drive 10 or even 20 mph over the speed limit, while others mosey along at 25 in a 55-mph zone. Both speedballs and slowpokes cause accidents.

c.   Society encourages young people to drink. For one thing, youngsters learn early that their parents and other relatives find alcohol consumption a necessity on birthdays, anniversaries, and graduations. They see their parents buying scotch to give as presents to clients and ordering liquor by the case for business functions. Memorial Day, Independence Day, and other national holidays also cause adults to break out the Budweiser, the Johnnie Walker, and even the Champagne. But the place where youngsters see alcohol depicted most enticingly is on television. Prime-time shows, like major sports events and popular sitcoms, are typically sponsored by beer and wine commercials and show healthy, jubilant people drinking liquor and having the time of their lives.

3.   The major flaws in each paragraph are indicated below.

a.   This paragraph lacks unity (U). Sentences five and nine ("Of course, participants' observations. . ."; "Such findings underscore. . .") are digressions from the main point.

b.   The support consists of the same point about brain size repeated over and over (R). The paragraph needs tightening.

c.   A problem in coherence (C) is caused by the lack of a transition between the first and second sentences, as well as by insufficient transitions to signal the second and third steps that adults can take to reduce their cholesterol level. Unity (U) is spoiled by the digression of the fifth sentence ("Physicians warn . . ."). The placement of the sixth sentence ("for those unwilling . . .") leads to another problem in coherence (C). Since this sentence develops the point about vegetarianism, it should go after the third sentence ("Since only foods . . ."), the sentence that first discusses vegetarianism.

4. Here is one way to revise the paragraph. (Transitional signals are italicized.)

As a camp counselor this past summer, I learned that leading young children is different from leading people your own age. I was president of my high school Ecology Club, *and* I ran it democratically. *When* we wanted to bring a speaker to the school, we decided to do a fund-raiser. I solicited ideas from everybody, *and then* we got together to figure out which was best. It became obvious that a raffle with prizes donated by local merchants was the most profitable. *So,* everybody got behind the effort.

This summer, on the other hand, I learned that little kids operate differently. *With them*, I had to be more of a boss than a democratic leader. *Once*, I took suggestions from the group on the main activity of the day. Everyone *then* voted for the best suggestion. Some kids got especially upset, *especially* those whose ideas were voted down. *As a result*, I learned to make the suggestions myself *and* allow the children to vote on them. *That way,* no one was overly attached to any of the suggestions. *Usually*, they felt the outcome of the voting was fair, *and* I basically got to be in charge.

5. Below are the patterns of development implied by each topic sentence.

Thesis: The college should make community service a requirement for graduation.

Definition	"Mandatory community service" is a fairly new and often misunderstood concept.
Narration	Here's the story of one student's community involvement.
Illustration	Indeed, a single program offers students numerous opportunities.
Cause-Effect	Such involvement can have a real impact on students' lives.
Comparison-Contrast	However, the college could adopt two very different approaches—one developed by a university, the other by a community college.
Argumentation-Persuasion	In any case, the college should begin exploring the possibility of making community service a graduation requirement.

37

9. It's a good idea to have students share their analysis of Harriet's first draft with each other in small groups. Such group discussion can help students understand all the ways in which Harriet's draft is working well.

    Here are the strengths of Harriet's draft:

    — An explicit statement of the thesis appears at the end of the introductory paragraph: "But being a parent today is much more difficult because nowadays parents have to shield/protect kids from lots of things, like distractions from schoolwork, from sexual material, and from dangerous situations."

    — Numerous details and examples are provided to support the development of the three points.

    — The essay follows the emphatic organizational pattern established in the thesis: "distractions from schoolwork, from sexual material, and from dangerous situations."

    The essay does have some problems, however, besides those Harriet noted as she wrote. For example:

    — The first body paragraph lacks unity because it contains a digression: the sentence beginning, "Unfortunately, though. . . ."

    — The second paragraph contains a digression at the end: "The situation has gotten so out of hand that maybe the government should establish guidelines. . . ."

    — The third-paragraph organization could be improved by using chronological order, beginning with little children, moving to slightly older children, and ending with teenagers.

    — The conclusion contains a vague reference to a fictional character; this unexpected allusion dilutes the impact of the ending.

ANSWERS FOR CHAPTER 7
"REVISING OVERALL MEANING, STRUCTURE, AND PARAGRAPH DEVELOPMENT" (p. 79)

Below we provide suggested responses to selected activities at the end of Chapter 7 (pp. 88–90). In many cases, other responses are possible.

1. Students profit from working in a group on this activity; if you have students work alone, then set aside some time for them to share their evaluations of the draft. If students worked on Harriet's draft for Activity 9 on page 93, they may wish to refer to their notes.

    Here are the problems, in addition to the ones she noted as she wrote, that Harriet will have to correct as she revises her essay.

    — The first body paragraph lacks unity because it contains a digression: The sentence beginning "Unfortunately, though . . ." has nothing to do with her thesis.

    — The second paragraph contains a digression at the end: "The situation has gotten so out of hand that maybe the government should establish guidelines. . . ."

    — The third paragraph's organization could be improved by using chronological order, beginning with little children, moving to slightly older children, and ending with teenagers.

    — The conclusion contains a vague reference to a fictional character; this unexplained allusion dilutes the impact of the ending.

3. The annotations below describe some of the essay's problems in meaning, structure, and development.

The Extended School Day

Imagine a seven-year-old whose parents work until five each night. When she arrives home after school, she is on her own. She's a good girl, but still *a lot of things could happen.* She could *get into trouble* just by *being* curious. Or, *something could happen through no fault of her own.* All over the country, there are many "latch-key" children like this little girl. Some way must be found to deal with the problem. One suggestion is to keep elementary schools open longer than they now are. *There are many advantages to this idea.*

Parents wouldn't have to be in a state of uneasiness about whether their child is safe and happy at home. *They wouldn't get uptight about whether their children's needs are being met. They also wouldn't have to feel guilty because they are not able to help a child with homework. The longer day would make it possible for the teacher to provide such help.* Extended school hours would also relieve families of the financial burden of hiring a home sitter. *As my family learned, having a sitter can wipe out the budget.* And, having a sitter doesn't necessarily eliminate all problems. Parents still have the hassle of worrying about whether the person will show up and be reliable.

It's a fact of life that many children dislike school, which is a sad commentary on the state of education in this country. Even so, the longer school day would benefit children as well. *Obviously, the dangers of their being home alone after school would disappear because by the time the bus dropped them off after the longer school day, at least one parent would be home. The unnameable horrors feared by parents would not have a chance to happen.* Instead, the children would be in school, under trained

Marginal notes (left column):

Vague phrases.

These should be more specific.

Support is weak, repetitive. 2nd point belongs in next paragraph.

Support too personal, inadequate.

Digression.

Support repeats ideas already discussed.

40

supervision. There, they would have a chance to work on subjects that give them trouble. *In contrast, when my younger brother had difficulty with subtraction in second grade, he had to struggle alone because there wasn't enough time to give him the help he needed.* The longer day would also give children a chance to participate in extracurricular activities. They could join a science club, play on a softball team, sing in a school chorus, take an art class. *Because school districts are trying to save money, they often cut back on such extracurricular activities. They don't realize how important such experiences are.*

Finally, the longer school day would *also benefit teachers.* Having more hours in each day would relieve them of *a lot of pressure. This longer work day would obviously require schools to increase teachers' pay. The added salary would be an incentive for teachers to stay in the profession.*

Implementing an extended school day would be expensive, but I feel that many communities would willingly finance its costs because it provides benefits to parents, children, and even teachers. *Young children, home alone, wondering whether to watch another TV show or wander outside to see what's happening, need this longer school day now.*

Support too personal, inadequate.

Here support is specific.
Irrelevant support.

Vague. Give specifics.

Digression.

Digression.

Good summary.

Strong concluding image.

ANSWERS FOR CHAPTER 8
"REVISING SENTENCES AND WORDS" (p. 91)

Below are suggested responses to selected activities at the end of Chapter 8 (pp. 114–16). In many cases, other responses are possible.

1. Below are possible revisions of the sentences. Other versions are possible.

   a. Before subletting an apartment, a person should have a formal sublet contract.

   b. High-school students often deny liking poetry because they fear the mockery of others.

   c. Since college students are rare in my neighborhood, going to college gave me instant status.

   d. Many people observed that the new wing of the library resembles several nearby historical buildings.

3. The revisions below show one way the sentences could be made more emphatic.

   a. Most of us find it difficult to deal with rude salespeople. (Important item last)

   b. "I'll solve all your problems," promises the politician. (Inverted order)

   c. In the movies, we meet the gold digger, the dangerous vixen, and the "girl next door." Female stereotypes all. (Fragment)

   d. Wise teachers encourage discussion of controversial issues in the classroom. (Important item first)

4. Here is a version of the paragraph that eliminates murkiness and gets straight to the point. Other versions might work equally well.

   Since its founding, our student senate has had one main goal: to improve its student services. Two years ago, consultants from the National Council of Student Governing Boards agreed with the senate that its services were basically strong but also felt that additional funding from the administration would further improve student services. This has turned out to be true; services have significantly improved in the last fifteen months since the administration began contributing more money.

5. Here are some ways to use each word in a sentence that reinforces its connotations. Other versions are possible.

    a. On her chubby legs, the toddler stiffly lurched across the room.

        Proud of her voluptuous figure, the bride-to-be asked the dressmaker to lower the neckline and tighten the bodice of her gown.

        The portly lawyer eased himself into his desk chair and slowly went over the will with his client.

    b. The engaged couple strolled on the riverbank, breathing in the fragrance of the spring blooms.

        Dripping wet under their uniforms, the mail carriers trudged determinedly through the summer heat.

        Loitering near the liquor store, the vacant-eyed man beseeched passers-by for money to buy a sandwich and soup.

    c. The students were in turmoil over the suspension of the class president for cheating on an exam.

        The demonstration turned into anarchy as bands of youths began throwing rocks, robbing vendors, and smashing car windows.

        When the "Sold Out" sign was posted, the movie fans created a hubbub by jeering the manager and jostling each other.

8. The examples below show some ways to enliven the sentences.

    a. With a fever of 101 degrees, I shivered and coughed my way through the tour of the California wineries.

    b. In his new silver convertible, the balding middle-aged man glided to a halt at the crowded intersection.

    c. Shifting in their seats, the math students doodled on their notebooks and restlessly tapped their pencils.

    d. Natasha Miles, the seasoned network reporter, put on a shocked face and assumed a hushed tone as she announced the crash of the international flight.

43

9. Below is a possible revision of the paragraph.

    The situation at Paul Godfrey's farm illustrates the problem of rural vandalism. Godfrey estimates that motorcyclists speeding over his land the past few weekends have destroyed over three acres of his crops. Such vandalism results from the suburbs encroaching on rural areas.

10. Here are nonsexist versions of the sentences.

    a. The manager of a convenience store has to guard the cash register carefully.

    b. When I broke my arm in a car accident, a nurse, aided by a physician's assistant, treated my injury.

    c. All of us should contact our congressional representatives if we're not happy with their performances.

    d. The chemistry professors agree that students shouldn't have to buy their own Bunsen burners.

ACTIVITIES FOR CHAPTER 9
"EDITING AND PROOFREADING" (p. 117)

Below we provide a suggested response to a selected activity at the end of Chapter 9 (p. 125). Other versions are possible.

1. Here is a corrected version of the letter.

    Dear Mr. Eno:

    As a sophomore at Harper College, I will be returning home to Brooktown this June, hoping to find a job for the summer. I would prefer a position that would give me further experience in the retail field. I have heard from my friend, Sarah Snyder, that you are hiring college students as assistant managers. I would be greatly interested in such a position.

    I have quite a bit of experience in retail sales, having worked after school in a Dress Place shop at Mason Mall, Pennsylvania. I started there as a sales clerk; by my second year, I was serving as assistant manager.

    I am reliable and responsible and truly enjoy sales work. Mary Carver, the owner of the Dress Place, can verify my qualifications. She has been my supervisor for two years.

    I will be visiting Brooktown from April 25 to 30. I hope to have an opportunity to speak to you about possible summer jobs at that time, and will be available for an interview at your convenience. Thank you for your consideration.

    Sincerely,

    Joan Ackerman

ANSWERS FOR CHAPTER 10
"DESCRIPTION" (p. 126)

OPENING COMMENTS

Some colleagues tell us they prefer to omit description when they teach freshman writing. Emphasizing the analytic side of exposition, they consider descriptive writing a digression, a luxury in an already crowded syllabus. To them, descriptive writing belongs in a creative-writing course, not in freshman composition. On the other hand, some instructors *do* include description, but they discuss it after narration.

We feel that descriptive writing should be included in freshman composition. And we've found that description can be covered before narration with excellent results. In other words, we recommend that description be the first pattern studied in the course.

Why do we feel this way? For one thing, when students begin by writing descriptive essays, they learn the importance of specific details, and they start to develop the habit of observation. (The sensory chart illustrated on page 134 is one way to encourage such attention to detail.) Also, since descriptive writing depends on creating a dominant impression, description helps students understand the concept of focus early in the semester.

Descriptive writing also teaches students to select details that enhance an essay's central point. Finally—and most importantly—students can discover real pleasure in writing descriptive pieces. They are challenged by the possibility that they can make readers feel as they do about a subject. They enjoy using words to share a place, person, or object that has personal significance to them. Every semester, we have students who admit that descriptive writing changed their attitude toward composition. For the first time, they see that writing, though difficult, can be rewarding and fun.

The selections in this chapter represent a wide range of techniques found in descriptive writing. Angelou's essay ("Sister Flowers") demonstrates the power of sensory details, while students will find David Helvarg's "The Storm This Time," about the effects of Hurricane Katrina on the Gulf Coast, to be compelling, dealing, as it does, with a recent event of such magnitude. That essay also gives students the chance to compare photographs with written descriptions. And the imagistic power of Parks's essay ("Flavio's Home") dramatizes the way vivid sensory details support a dominant impression.

ACTIVITIES: DESCRIPTION

Below we provide suggested responses to selected activities at the end of Chapter 10. Of course, other approaches are possible.

Prewriting Activities (p. 139)

1. There are many ways to use description in these two essays; below we've listed some of the possibilities. In classroom use of this activity, we suggest you have students share their responses. They'll be surprised and often delighted to discover their neighbors have devised quite different uses for description in the essays. Sharing and comparing such prewriting conveys the invaluable point that writers are individual and their writing is unique.

   Topic: How students get burned out
   Describe ineffective studying methods: cramming, skimming
   Describe student with six courses struggling with homework
   Draw portrait of aloof professor assigning too-difficult work
   Describe student working and carrying full load

   Topic: Being a spendthrift is better than being frugal
   Describe allure of some purchase: dress, sneakers, etc.
   Describe appeal of shopping center or mall
   Describe gourmet meal at expensive restaurant

   Topic: Being a spendthrift is worse than being frugal
   Describe shocked clerk ringing up your large purchase
   Describe empty pockets and meager lunches after a spree
   Describe sleepless night after charging a lot

Revising Activities (p. 139)

4. Here are some possible ways to revise the sentences to create distinct, contrasting moods. Other versions are, of course, possible.

   a. Around the filthy, lopsided table slouched four grubby, droopy-eyed old men.

   Alert and eagle-eyed, the four natty old poker players sat tensely around the felt-topped table.

b. Enticed by media attention to the movie's special effects, hordes of boisterous teenagers thronged the street outside the theater showing *Race to Doom*.

Snaking down the alley beside the theater, a line of silent, slouch-hatted customers waited to see the notorious film.

c. The skinny 12-year-old girl teetered, wobbled, and finally tripped as she walked into church in her first pair of high heels.

With head held high, hips swaying, and eyes roving to see if anyone noticed, Mary Beth strolled down Main Street in her first pair of high heels.

5. Here are some ways to revise the sentences. Other versions are possible, of course. Encourage students to avoid other similar clichés ("dull as dust," "jealous as sin," and so on).

a. The workers were as quiet as children waiting for recess.

The café cooks were suddenly quiet as water waiting to boil.

b. My brother used to become as envious as a 4-year-old at someone else's birthday party if I had a date and he didn't.

My brother would look as if he just drank sour milk if I had a date and he didn't.

c. Andrea is as proud as an Olympic champion of her new Girl Scout uniform.

The little girl dressed in her new Girl Scout uniform twirled like a music-box ballerina.

d. The professor is as dull as a dead snail.

Professor Tomari is as dull as an iceberg-lettuce sandwich on white bread.

6. We suggest that you offer your students the chance to read each other's revisions of this paragraph. Such exposure to the versions of others helps them see a variety of possibilities in improving a piece of writing.

Here are the main problems in the paragraph:

— Details about driving on Route 334 are irrelevant and should be eliminated.

— Statement that car has been "washed and waxed" detracts attention from arrival at farm.

— Short, choppy sentences could be combined with others nearby: "Its paint must have worn off decades ago"; "They were dented and windowless." For example, such combined sentences might read: "Then I headed for the dirt-colored barn, its roof full of huge, rotted holes"; "As I rounded the bushes, I saw the dirt-colored house, its paint worn off decades ago"; "A couple of dented, windowless, dead-looking old cars were sprawled in front of the barn."

— Spatial order is broken by placing description of house in between details about what is near the barn.

SISTER FLOWERS

Maya Angelou

Questions for Close Reading (p. 144)

1. The dominant impression is implied and can be stated as, "The care and attention of a loving mentor is crucial to a child's healthy development, particularly in times of crisis." In addition, Angelou seeks to draw a portrait of beloved Mrs. Flowers, the essence of whom Angelou expresses when she writes, "[Mrs. Flowers] was one of the few gentlewomen I have ever known, and has remained throughout my life the measure of what a human being can be" (paragraph 5).

2. Mrs. Flowers represents for Angelou the gentility and sophistication as well as the benevolence that she has read about in novels and seen in films but has never encountered firsthand, especially not among her fellow townspeople. She says "She appealed to me because she was like people I had never met personally" (11) and calls her "the aristocrat of Black Stamps" (2). Flowers's stunning beauty and impeccable grooming (2–4) powerfully impress Angelou, who lives in a community of relatively poor and minimally educated people. Still more fascinating is Flowers's refined grace (12), dazzling intellect, and stirring eloquence (22), all of which inspire

49

Angelou to strive for a standard she previously thought accessible only to privileged whites. Angelou reflects, "She made me proud to be Negro, just by being herself" (11). Most of all, Angelou is profoundly honored and grateful that Flowers would not only spend time with her but also impart to her the "lessons for living" that would form the foundation of Angelou's subsequent existence.

3. Angelou humorously describes her frustration and embarrassment when witnessing her unrefined Momma speaking to the highly educated and proper Mrs. Flowers. In particular, Angelou is ashamed of Momma's calling Mrs. Flowers "*Sister* Flowers." To the young Angelou, such an informal appellation is inconsistent with what she considers the obvious superiority of her elegant neighbor. In Angelou's opinion, "Mrs. Flowers deserved better than to be called Sister" (7). Worse still is Momma's flawed grammar as she speaks to Flowers; Angelou agonizes over Momma's incorrect and missing verbs and says that she "hated [Momma] for showing her ignorance to Mrs. Flowers" (7). Despite Angelou's intense embarrassment over Momma, Momma and Flowers share an amicable and mutually respectful friendship—a fact that perplexes Angelou, who calls their relationship "strange" (6). Flowers does not object to Momma's calling her "Sister" and in fact might be pleased to be included in the community of women; similarly, Momma feels enough kinship with Flowers to call her "Sister." The two women often engage in "intimate conversation" with each other (10), and it is implied that Momma has asked Flowers's assistance in mentoring the withdrawn young Angelou. Years later, Angelou finally realizes that Momma and Flowers were indeed "as alike as sisters, separated only by formal education" (7), a notion reinforced by Flowers's insistence that Angelou appreciate the wisdom of "mother wit," such as that of Momma (35).

4. The first significant lesson Mrs. Flowers teaches Angelou is about the beauty and power of language. In the process of convincing young Angelou that she needs to participate verbally in class, Flowers explains that "it is language alone which separates [man] from the lower animals," a notion that was "a totally new idea" to Angelou (23). Soon after, in a statement that Angelou remembers as "valid and poetic," Flowers says, "It takes the human voice to infuse [words] with the shades of deeper meaning" (24). Flowers's melodic, invigorating reading of *A Tale of Two Cities* convincingly illustrates to Angelou the vast power of words. (Clearly, this lesson had a tremendous impact on Angelou, presently a renowned writer not only of novels but also of poetry.) The next important lesson concerns the nature of wisdom and intelligence. Probably perceiving Angelou's embarrassment at Momma's lack of refinement, Flowers informs her that many unschooled people are more knowledgeable and intelligent than some highly educated scholars. "Mother wit," she asserts, is every bit as valuable (if not more so) as book knowledge, for it contains

"the collective wisdom of generations" (35). Flowers's lesson on knowledge is summed up when she advises Angelou to "always be intolerant of ignorance but understanding of illiteracy" (35). Following this advice, it seems likely that young Angelou would think twice before judging Momma harshly again. Beyond these explicitly stated lessons, Angelou also receives the invaluable understanding that she is a unique and likable individual worthy of the attention of an exemplary woman, a realization that will help rebuild her wounded self-confidence.

5. *taut* (2): tightly pulled or strained
    voile (2): a light, sheer fabric
    benign (4): kind and gentle
    unceremonious (8): informal
    gait (8): particular way of walking
    moors (11): broad area of open land, often containing patches of wetness
    incessantly (11): continuing without interruption
    scones (11): small biscuitlike pastries
    crumpets (11): small, round cakelike breads
    heath (11): large area of land containing low-growing shrubs
    chifforobe (17): tall piece of furniture containing drawers and space for hanging clothes
    sacrilegious (17): disrespectful of something held sacred
    infuse (24): to introduce into as if by pouring
    couched (35): expressed
    aura (42): an invisible atmosphere seeming to surround something or someone

Questions About the Writer's Craft (p. 146)

1. Angelou relies primarily on visual and occasionally on both tactile and auditory impressions to convey Flowers's "aristocratic" appearance. In paragraph 2, Angelou describes her graceful bearing that never evidences extremes of weather and her thin frame, which lacks the "taut look of wiry people." Flowers's attire is the next object of Angelou's attention as she observes the elegant woman's airy "printed voile dresses," "flowered hats," and gloves (2). Angelou then describes Flowers's "rich black" complexion, comparing it to the visual and tactile image of an easily peeled plum (3). Angelou also details Flowers's "slow dragging" smile (15), thin black lips, "even, small white teeth" (4) and "soft yet carrying voice" (6). Later she mentions Flowers's "easy gait" (8). In general, Angelou organizes these details of Flowers's appearance spatially, moving first from her physical carriage and attire up to her face

and zeroing in on her smile (although she returns to Flowers's "easy gait" later in the essay).

To describe her reaction when she first arrived at Flowers's home, Angelou invokes the sense of smell when, for example, she cites the "sweet scent of vanilla" (29). She then draws upon the visual sense to describe what she observes: "browned photographs" and "white, freshly done curtains" (32). The next part of the visit calls upon the visual as well as the taste faculty as Angelou describes eating Flowers's delectable cookies ("flat round wafers, slightly browned on the edges and butter-yellow in the center") and drinking the refreshing cold lemonade (34). The tactile sense is appealed to when she mentions the "rough crumbs" of the cookies scratching against her jaw (34). And the sense of sound is evoked as Angelou remembers Flowers's reading voice "cascading" and "nearly singing" (37). Overall, Angelou organizes this last set of richly textured sensory impressions spatially as well as chronologically; that is, she presents the details as she moves through the house and as the afternoon progresses.

2. The first figure of speech is the simile Angelou uses in comparing herself to an old biscuit (1). This image establishes young Angelou's shame and withdrawal following the rape; indeed, her depression is what prompts Flowers to find time to talk with the child. Angelou then employs a series of striking figures of speech to describe Flowers's character and demeanor. The most powerful appear in paragraph 11. There Angelou provides a series of similes using "like" to compare Flowers with the gentle, elegant "women in English novels who walked the moors . . . with their loyal dogs racing at a respectful distance" and "the women who sat in front of roaring fireplaces, drinking tea incessantly from silver trays full of scones and crumpets." The final simile of the paragraph is an implied one; although it lacks "like," it deliberately mirrors the structure of the previous two similes: "Women who walked over the 'heath' and read morocco-bound books and had two last names divided by a hyphen." The function of these similes comparing Flowers to female British gentility is to reinforce the notion of Flowers as "the aristocrat of Black Stamps" (2). The basis of Flowers's allure for Angelou is her otherworldly elegance and sophistication, particularly when juxtaposed with the ordinary citizens of Black Stamps. That this elegant and gracious woman actually seeks out the young Angelou is enough to transform the child from an "old biscuit" into one who excitedly runs down the road, flush with the pleasure of being liked.

3. The technique of imagined conversation injects humor into Angelou's portrait of herself as a child, while also allowing readers greater insight into her character by giving them access to her mental processes. The young Angelou's imagined scoldings of Momma resoundingly illustrate her embarrassment with "uncouth"

52

Momma. Here Angelou seems caught between two worlds: that of "backwards" Momma and Black Stamps and that of education and opportunity seemingly offered by the outside world. As Mrs. Flowers instructs, however, much wisdom resides in "mother wit" like Momma's, and given this lesson young Angelou would probably be led to reevaluate her embarrassed attitude toward Momma.

4. From Angelou's very first statement about Mrs. Flowers, it is apparent that race is a significant facet of life in Angelou's town. Flowers is said to be "the aristocrat of Black Stamps," a statement that draws its power from the notion that aristocrats have traditionally been white. This depiction of Flowers as being uniquely regal is heightened by Angelou's comparing her to British female gentry (11) and by her observation that Flowers behaves differently from the average "Negro woman" (14) in town. Most significantly, Angelou states that Flowers made her "proud to be a Negro, just by being herself" (11), a difficult feat given the racist climate of the day. The town's appellation, "Black Stamps" (12), implies the existence of a "White Stamps," a fact later confirmed when Angelou mentions "powhitefolks" (13). Angelou indicates that no Negro, not even the elegant Flowers, is immune to the disrespect of the town's self-aggrandizing poor whites. Indeed, even Angelou's reverence for Flowers "would have been shattered like the unmendable Humpty-Dumpty" (13) if the "powhitefolks" had called this revered idol by her first name, Bertha. Angelou lives in a world that would sanction such racially inspired disrespect and insult. In paragraph 42, Angelou refers to "Southern bitter wormwood," a subtle reference to racism. In such a world, it is difficult for a black child—especially one so traumatized and wounded—to develop a strong sense of self. But that is just what the encounter with Mrs. Flowers achieves; it makes young Angelou "feel proud" to be a Negro, and with that comes the loosening of trauma's hold on her.

THE STORM THIS TIME

David Helvarg

Questions for Close Reading (p. 152)

1. Helvarg does not explicitly state his thesis until the end of the essay. In paragraphs 26 and 27, he says that the hurricanes of 2005 caused a massive coastal environmental disaster for which people were unprepared and from which they must recover in a more environmentally sound way than in the past.

2. The subject of the section "Urban Floodplain" is the damage done in the city of New Orleans itself. Helvarg drives to New Orleans from Baton Rouge and tours the Lakeview section, which had been flooded, and the central business district, which had not. He describes Lakeview as a disaster area and the central business district as a staging area for emergency personnel. In the last paragraph, he explains the purpose of his trip—to travel around the "new urban landscape" of the region to view the effects of Katrina. The remainder of the essay describes his trip throughout the Gulf region.

3. The activity that shows life going on as usual appears in paragraph 24, where Helvarg describes how people attending a football game in Baton Rouge will be allowed to return home after curfew as long as they show their ticket stubs at the roadblocks. This is the last description in the essay, before Helvarg turns to the statement of his thesis and conclusion. Its purpose is to provide a hopeful contrast to all the accumulated details of destruction that preceded it and to symbolically point to the future, in which people will again take up their normal activities.

4. According to one dictionary, "eco" means "habitat" or "environment," and "geek" means "a person of an intellectual bent who is disapproved of." In this paragraph, Helvarg is characterizing himself as a person too caught up in environmental issues, worrying about the threats to birds and swamps rather than the threats to people's livelihoods caused by the destruction of the casinos. An "eco-geek," therefore, is a person who focuses on environmental issues at the expense of (more important) human issues. A related neologism is "tree hugger."

5. *consortium* (1): a group formed to perform a task beyond the capacity of any one member
    infiltrating (4): gradually entering an area through small gaps or by filtering through
    Woodstock (5): a 1969 rock festival attended by thousands who camped out together
    salvage (8): to save, especially from ruin
    ruptured (10): burst
    antebellum (11): pre-Civil War
    festooned (13): hung
    storm surge (16): seawater pushed on shore by the force of high winds
    adjuster (18): a representative of an insurance company who determines the amount the company must pay on a claim
    mercenary (23): one who works only for money, especially a hired soldier

Questions About the Writer's Craft (p. 152)

1. Helvarg uses a spatial organization in this essay, traveling from place to place and describing what he sees. Helvarg keeps the reader oriented as to his movements by describing how he travels from one place to another. For example, at the beginning of the essay he arrives in Baton Rouge by plane, then he drives south toward New Orleans, where he begins to see destruction when he is near the New Orleans airport. In paragraph 4, he tells the reader he is driving into Lakeview. He describes Lakeview and then drives to downtown New Orleans, the site of the next descriptive section. In paragraph 7, he has crossed the Mississippi west of New Orleans into Algiers; in paragraph 8, he is back in Lakeview. In the next section, paragraph 10, he drives through Plaquemines Parish; in paragraph 12, he is "approaching the Empire Bridge." Helvarg provides similar transitional information about his travels as he describes each place he visits. It's possible to trace his trip on a map from these transitional cues, which provide the reader with a sense of being on the ground with him.

2. Helvarg describes smells and tastes as well as sights. For example, in paragraph 4, Helvarg describes both the smell he expected (the smell of death as in a war zone) and the smell he actually smelled—"the smell of a dead city, like dried cow pies and mold with a stinging chemical aftertaste." In that description, he includes the sense of taste as well as the sense of smell. Another description that focuses on the sense of smell is in paragraph 9, in which Helvarg describes Bob Chick's house as "reeking of mold and rotted cat food." He says, "I try not to breathe too deeply." These descriptions are particularly vivid because they engage a sense other than the sense of sight, giving the description more than one dimension.

3. Helvarg compares the post-Katrina Gulf Coast to a war zone in paragraphs 4 and 24, helping the reader understand the scale and randomness of the destruction. Since a war zone is full of damaged or destroyed buildings and other property, as well as dead or wounded people, the images this comparison conveys contribute to the dominant impression of the essay, which is that property and environmental damage was widespread, serious, and random. Helvarg points out in paragraph 24 that the analogy fails if you consider the death toll, which was less for Katrina than in a typical war zone.

4. The photograph of the marked doorway (p. 94) provides more information than the author gives in paragraph 6. In paragraph 6, Helvarg describes in general how rescue workers indicate that a house has been searched, but he does not describe a particular door. The photo specifically illustrates the general procedure that the workers were

55

following, so its impact goes beyond the impact of the rather vague verbal description. In the case of the photo of Bob Chick (p. 95), an argument can be made that it is superfluous because Helvarg has captured Chick's situation vividly in paragraphs 8 and 9. Furthermore, his description of the photo in paragraph 9 ("He's wearing a mask, rubber boots and gloves, but still manages to give an expressive shrug of resignation when I take his picture") is so accurate and complete that the photo simply confirms it. (On the other hand, one can argue that the photo of Bob makes him a symbol of all the people struggling to recover from Katrina and that is enough to warrant the photo's inclusion. Note that this argument has nothing to do with the author's powers of description, which are considerable.)

If students were writing this essay, they might or might not include the photos that accompany it, although it's likely that most would include them since photos provide visual breaks from the text and show actual scenes of destruction and real people, both of which help to bring the subject to life. Students might indicate they would use the photos to refresh their memories of what they saw as they were writing the essay. Or they might cut the verbal description of a photo's particular scene from the text and convey those particular details via the photo and caption rather than in the main part of the essay. If there were more photos, some students might even turn this piece into a photo essay, in which the photos dominate and the text supports them.

FLAVIO'S HOME

Gordon Parks

Questions for Close Reading (p. 159)

1. The dominant impression is implied. While Parks is explicit about his overall attitude to poverty in paragraph 1, this material is not the thesis. Rather, the dominant impression pertains more specifically to Flavio. It might be stated as, "Even in the midst of the worst afflictions of poverty, the human spirit survives in certain optimistic, energetic, caring individuals such as the 12-year-old boy Flavio."

2. In Flavio's family, there's no sense of understanding or emotional nurturing of children; rather, all the family's focus is on survival. At 12, Flavio is the oldest child of eight, ranging down to infancy. His parents work, leaving him with the care of the household and the other children. His mother is a laundress who washes clothes in the river, and the father sells bleach and kerosene at a small stand. The parents seem

56

too fatigued to be interested in their children; the father relates to them primarily by giving commands and demanding instant obedience.

3. The neighborhood is on a steep, difficult-to-climb mountainside. Paragraphs 2, 3, 14, and 21 describe the sights and sounds Parks encounters on this arduous climb. He reports encountering "mud trails, jutting rock, slime-filled holes and shack after shack propped against the slopes on shaky pilings." The trail is also crowded with people going up and down; "bare feet and legs with open sores climbed above us," Parks writes (21). While the mountainside is "a maze of shacks," from it one can see the beaches with the "gleaming white homes of the rich" (2). Flavio's home is described in paragraph 6. It is a one-room shack, six by ten feet, constructed of miscellaneous boards with numerous gaps in the walls. The wooden floor is rotten and spotted with light leaking in through the holes in the roof. One corner has a hole dug for a toilet; it lets out onto the side of the mountain.

4. Flavio seems well aware that hosts should not eat in front of guests, but he is probably afraid that his domineering and skeptical father would be angered by an offer to join them. He may also be reluctant to be a good host because there isn't enough food to go around; his family lives on the brink of starvation, and he knows the guests do not need the food as much as his family. Parks and Gallo understand that Flavio really can't or shouldn't offer food, and so they refuse.

5. *barrios* (1): Latin-American term for districts
    jacaranda (2): tropical tree having clusters of pale purple flowers
    jaundiced (3): yellow toned, ill with a disorder of the bile (liver)
    spigot (14): faucet

Questions About the Writer's Craft (p. 159)

1. The dominant impression we receive of Flavio is of a child who is ravaged by poverty yet possesses an open and persevering soul. Throughout the essay, Parks reveals Flavio's character by describing what Flavio says and does rather than what the boy is like as a person. He gives us numerous details of Flavio's physical appearance (3, 11, 23), pointing out the boy's thinness, sticklike limbs, sunken eyes, jaundiced coloring, wrenching coughs, and filthy, skimpy clothing. Parks also notices one other thing—the brilliant smile that instantly crosses Flavio's face as he sees the strangers. Parks details each time the smile occurs—when the boy opens the door (4), offers food (10), carries Parks's camera (22), recovers from a coughing spell (23), and enters the doctor's office (29). The nobility of the boy's spirit also comes through

in other details: his competence in household tasks and care of his siblings (5, 7, 9, 23–26) and his refusal to let Parks carry wood for him (22).

2. Parks describes how household tasks are made difficult by the need to conserve water. In paragraph 7, we see the process by which Flavio gets the rice washed, the children bathed, and the floor scrubbed, with only one pan of water. In paragraph 10, the boy serves dinner, a task complicated by the existence of only three plates and two spoons. He prepares breakfast in paragraph 23, making a fire and reheating the dinner. These processes add to the dominant impression of Flavio by showing us his discipline, ingenuity, and steadiness.

3. Parks conveys strong sensory images in such phrases as "a rusted, bent top of an old gas range," "a piece of tin," "grimy walls," "a patchwork of misshapen boards," "other shacks below stilted against the slopes," "rotting," "layers of grease and dirt," "shafts of light slanting down," "spaces in the roof," and "large hole." We are able to flow from image to image because Parks uses numerous transitions of spatial organization: "beneath it," "between them," "under layers," "slanting down through," "in the far corner," and "beneath that hole." Parks also uses a clear organizational pattern in the description; he begins describing the room with one important object, the stove. Then he moves from the walls to the floor; he ingeniously indicates the roof's condition by pointing out the sunlight dappling the floor from the holes above. He concludes by describing a hole in the "far corner" that serves as a toilet and that empties out onto the slope of the mountain. This detail, that the latrine empties essentially into thin air, conveys the precariousness and primitiveness of the home.

4. The effect of this scene is to dramatize the huge disparity between the rich and poor in Rio, between not only their dress but their emotional lives, the one basic and elemental, the other extravagant and romantic. The hotel lobby is filled with people dressed up for the evening in formal attire; Parks finds himself hoping the elevator will be empty since he has just been in the slums and is not very presentable. But a couple in evening clothes enter the elevator and embrace romantically, totally ignoring him. This action symbolizes the way in which the moneyed classes so easily ignore the "stink of the favela," even when it is right in the elevator with them.

ANSWERS FOR CHAPTER 11
"NARRATION" (p. 163)

OPENING COMMENTS

In our classes, we introduce narrative writing *after* description because we have found that descriptive writing helps students acquire many of the skills needed to write engaging narratives. For example, through descriptive writing, students discover the need to generate evocative details, use varied sentence structure, and establish a clear point of view.

At the start of the course, however, we often find students reluctant to write a narrative. Schooled to believe that lightning will strike them if they use "I" in an essay, they are more comfortable starting with description because it lends itself easily to the objective third-person point of view. (Obviously, both narration and description can use either the first or third person, but beginning writers tend to associate narration with the first and description with the third person.)

Even if it is not the first pattern covered, we suggest that narration be introduced near the beginning of the course. Everyone, after all, likes a good story. Also, most students have written narratives in high school and so feel comfortable tackling them in college. Despite some students' familiarity and seeming ease with the narrative pattern, it helps to keep in mind that narration requires a sophisticated repertoire of skills. Pacing, choice of details, telescoping of time, point of view—all offer a real challenge.

Students seem to have particular trouble understanding point of view. Because they tend to be more familiar with the first rather than the third person, we've found it useful to ask them to write two versions of the same narrative—one in the first and one in the third person. Such an assignment shows students how point of view changes a story and makes them aware of the advantages and limitation of each perspective.

Each narrative in this chapter is filled with drama and tension. In Audre Lorde's "Fourth of July," the author uses narration to explore the anger and confusion created by her parents' silence in regard to prejudice. Students will find special power in the conflicts underlying Orwell's "Shooting an Elephant." And Murray's "Someone's Mother" conveys the discomfort of an elderly woman who cannot remember where she lives but doesn't want her son to find out—again.

ACTIVITIES: NARRATION

Below we provide possible responses to selected activities at the end of Chapter 11. Of course, your students are bound to come up with their own inventive approaches.

Prewriting Activities (p. 176)

1. There are numerous ways to use narration to open these two essays. Below we've listed some of the possibilities. In going over this activity in class, we suggest you have students trade responses or read them aloud to each other, so that they are all aware of the diversity of responses to the assignment.

    Topic: The effect of insensitive teachers on young children

    > Teacher being sarcastic to student making a mistake
    > Teacher joking about student's clothing choices
    > Child's reading mistakes increasing as teacher corrects
    > Child crying after a teacher's cruel remark
    > Teacher punishing harshly for small transgression
    > Name-calling or labeling of a child for being different

    Topic: The importance of family traditions

    > Family seated at Sunday dinner
    > Sugary doughnuts for all at breakfast for a family birthday
    > Generations gathered at a holiday for a yearly reunion
    > Fourth of July kite flying with all the cousins
    > Gathering at year's end to view selected family videos

3. Here are some possible conflicts for each situation:

    a. Friend criticizes your food choices as unhealthy
        Friend embarrasses you by snacking on food throughout store

    b. College choice is on the other side of the country
        College choice does not offer the major your parents wish you to take

    c. Counterdemonstrators accost your group
        Some protestors break the law by trespassing and are arrested

60

d. Fighting the desire to go to the gym instead of studying
    Telling friends to be quiet or go away

Revising Activities (p. 177)

5. Here are some ways to revise the sentence sets to create first a negative connotation and then a positive connotation. Other versions are possible, of course.

    a. The raucous clanging of the bell signaled that the last day of lectures and homework was finally over.

        With a gentle dinging sound from the school bell, the last day of high school quietly ended.

    b. We strode over to admonish our neighbors for polluting the air with burning leaves.

        We had a neighborly chat with the Joneses, while the autumn leaves burned fragrantly in their yard.

    c. The sun slicing through my window jolted me upright in bed, and I was forced to admit that daylight had come.

        The lemony-yellow sunshine poured across my bed, and I sat up, grateful the new day was finally here.

6. It's a good idea to set aside some time for students to exchange their versions of the paragraph with others. Seeing how others handled the assignment can open their eyes to techniques they haven't thought of.

    Students should keep in mind as they revise that this is an introductory anecdote. It needs to be brief and pointed. Here are the main problems in the paragraph:

    — The reference to the type of car the writer was driving is irrelevant and should be deleted.

    — The speeding car should be described.

    — The description "The car didn't slow down . . ." is slow paced and indirect; rewrite to state that the car "sped. . . ."

61

— Description of car coming, light changing, couple crossing is too slow; condense and make more dramatic.

— "Dressed like models" is irrelevant, unless other details are added later in the paragraph to indicate how rumpled and bloody their clothes now are.

— The sentence about the man "jump[ing] to the shoulder" is short and choppy.

— Describe man's and woman's locations and injuries more visually, instead of saying he "wasn't hurt" but "it was clear she was."

— Narrator's calling police is a digression; condense events to get to the point: she died.

— Give more visual details of speeding car stopping, driver getting out, instead of saying he "looked terrible"; give us a picture of him drunk.

— Use his repeated offenses as a lead-in or stronger transition to the final sentence, the thesis.

THE FOURTH OF JULY

Audre Lorde

Questions for Close Reading (p. 180)

1. Here is one possible way of stating the essay's implied thesis: "Lorde's eighth-grade graduation was supposed to mark the end of her childhood. But it was her Fourth of July graduation-present trip to Washington, D.C., that truly marked the end of her innocence, because there she encountered the harsh reality of racism."

2. This picnic is Lorde's mother's idea of what it means to take care of her family, even to the extent that she provides different pickles (one type for the father, another type for the kids), wraps peaches separately so they won't bruise, and puts in a tin of rosewater for messy hands. Being a good mother also means packing the things your family enjoys, like "'marigolds' . . . from Cushman's Bakery . . . and rock-cakes from Newton's" (paragraph 4). All these domestic details of a caring mother

underscore the injustice, the horrific irony of the way the family is treated at the ice-cream counter. Although Lorde's mother probably believed in her heart that packing the picnic was a way to keep her family safe from food touched by the hands of strangers, more importantly, it was also a way to keep her children away from the racist situation they would most likely encounter in the railroad dining car. In short, these elaborate picnic preparations were evidence of the mother's avoidance of unpleasantness at all costs.

3. There are two reasons Lorde gives us for her inability to comprehend her parents' admonitions against white people. First of all, Lorde's parents never gave her any reasons; they just expected her "to know without being told" (7) the logic behind their warnings and the source of their feelings regarding white people. In addition, she has difficulty accepting such a dictate when her mother, as she tells us, "looked so much like one of those people we were never supposed to trust" (7). The fuzziness of the dictate leaves Lorde doubly vulnerable to the experience she encounters at the ice-cream counter.

4. In paragraphs 5 and 6, Lorde illustrates her mother's attempt to sidestep racism and her father's attempt to make up for it. By packing an elaborate picnic for the trip, Lorde's mother successfully avoids subjecting her family to the racism they would surely have encountered had they attempted to eat in the dining car. And when Lorde's sister is denied access to her own senior class trip because, truth be told, they would be staying in a hotel that "did not rent rooms to Negroes," Lorde's father tries to offset Phyllis's disappointment by planning a family trip instead. In paragraph 7, Lorde explains her parents' behavior more fully. She writes, "They handled it as a private woe. My mother and father believed that they could best protect their children from the realities of race in america and the fact of american racism by never giving them name, much less discussing their nature."

In the picture Lorde draws for us in paragraph 18, her family does not so much deal with the situation as ignore it. After the waitress delivered her message, Lorde tells us, "Straight-backed and indignant, one by one, my family got down from the counter stools and turned around and marched out of the store, quiet and outraged, as if we had never been Black before." But when she questions her parents about this obvious injustice, they don't answer her. In fact, they never address the incident, "not because they had contributed to it, but because they felt they should have anticipated it and avoided it" (19). Lorde gets increasingly angry not only because her parents do not share her heated emotions but also because they seem to accept responsibility for what happened. Also, her sisters mimic her parents' pretense of denial, and this invalidation of her response from all members of the family just heightens Lorde's fury and anger. Moreover, while she is given the freedom to articulate her fury in a letter to the president of the United States, because her father insists upon reviewing the letter before she sends it off we wonder whether she will be permitted to fully express her righteous rage.

5. *fabled* (1): famous; legendary
    injunction (7): order or demand
    progressive (8): favoring progress or reform
    dilated (9): enlarged
    vulnerable (9): unprotected
    travesty (10): a ridiculous representation of something
    decreed (13): ordered
    pretense (19): false appearance

Questions About the Writer's Craft (p. 181)

1. Lorde uses transitions of time and place to let us know when and where events occur. In the first sentence of the essay, Lorde establishes a general time frame when she writes that events occurred "on the edge of . . . summer." The final sentence of paragraph 1 narrows that time frame down to the Fourth of July. In paragraph 2, we learn that Lorde's family took the trip "during the day" and that it was made by train. We know that the train leaves New York City and passes through Philadelphia; Lorde writes, "I remember it was Philadelphia because I was disappointed not to have passed by the Liberty Bell" (3). In paragraphs 8 and 12, she signals the family's arrival at their destination ("In Washington, D.C., we had one large room with two double beds and an extra cot for me") as well as the family's movement out of the hotel to see the sites ("I spent the whole next day after Mass squinting up at the Lincoln Memorial"). Paragraph 13 reveals the passage of time ("Later that Washington afternoon my family and I walked back down Pennsylvania Avenue"), while paragraphs 15 and 16 set the scene at the ice-cream parlor ("Two blocks away from our hotel, the family . . . stopped . . . at a . . . soda fountain . . . . Corded and crisped and pinafored, the five of us seated ourselves one by one at the counter") and indicate Lorde's place in the scene ("There was I between my mother and father"). Paragraph 18 reveals the family's response to the waitress's refusal to serve them (". . . one by one, my family . . . got down from the counter . . . and marched out of the store"). That day ends with Lorde's writing a letter to the president of the United States, which her father promises she can type out on the "office typewriter next week" (19). The "whole rest of that trip," Lorde writes, she felt sick to her stomach (20).

64

2. In paragraphs 5–7, 9–11, and 19–20, Lorde moves from the events of the day to other discussions. Nevertheless, the information she provides in these instances is critical. The last sentence of paragraph 5 and the whole of paragraphs 6 and 7 are used to convey the way her parents handle racism and how their behavior affects her. Although the information in these paragraphs does not advance the narrative itself, what she reveals here has much to do with the experience she is describing. Her parents' failure to explain "the realities of race in america and the fact of american racism" leaves her open to the confusion and pain she feels while in Washington.

   In paragraphs 9–11, we learn that Lorde has trouble seeing clearly every summer; her eyes are unable to adjust to the "dazzling whiteness" of July. At first, this little aside about squinting seems arbitrary and unnecessary, but later we find that it is actually a metaphor for being blinded to racism: just as her parents "did not approve of sunglasses, nor of their expense" (thus forcing her to squint her way through each summer, never seeing clearly), they also did not approve of racism discussions, nor of the cost of exposing their children to the reality of racism (thus forcing Lorde into a sort of blindness that made the day of clarity all the more painful).

   In paragraph 19, Lorde tells us that her sisters, like her parents, behaved as though nothing was wrong with what happened in the ice-cream parlor. In fact, her whole family seemed to have a tacit agreement that denial was the best way to handle—or not handle—racism. Lorde feels alone in her inability to accept injustice. As a result, Washington, D.C., becomes a solid block of whiteness that makes her sick to her stomach, and the trip itself proves to be "[not] much of a graduation present after all" (20).

3. Lorde's use of the lowercase is appropriate. Given the soul-searing incident she experiences in Washington, D.C., the nation's capital, on the holiday commemorating that nation's Declaration of Independence and its promise of freedom and justice for all, the use of lowercase letters conveys her lack of respect for a country and a leader that fail to uphold those promises implied in the celebration of the Fourth of July.

4. In paragraph 20, Lorde repeats the word "white" over and over again: "The waitress was white, and the counter was white, and the ice cream I never ate in Washington, D.C., that summer I left childhood was white, and the white heat and the white pavement and the white stone monuments of my first Washington summer made me sick to my stomach for the whole rest of that trip and it wasn't much of a graduation present after all." Like Lorde, who feels overcome by the prevalence of racism, we too are overcome by the word "white" and can understand Lorde's experience: Racism is constant and exists everywhere.

SHOOTING AN ELEPHANT

George Orwell

Questions for Close Reading (p. 188)

1. Orwell's thesis is implied. One possible way of stating it is, "Imperialistic rulers must behave so as not to lose face or power over the populace, even if it means doing something against their better judgment."

2. Orwell felt pressured by the people, almost overwhelmed by their power over him through their mere presence. In theory, he explains at the start of the selection, he "was all for the Burmese and all against their oppressors, the British" (2). But in reality, Orwell says, he felt the common people of the country were "evil-spirited little beasts who tried to make my job impossible" (2). During the shooting incident the people were "happy and excited," and they watched him "as they would a conjurer about to perform a trick." He resentfully saw himself as having to spend his life "trying to impress the 'natives'" (7). He reports later that, as he fired a shot, the crowd emitted a "devilish roar of glee" (11). His choice of words shows that he resented and disliked the Burmese.

3. Orwell shoots the elephant because the two thousand native people standing behind him expect him to. They want vengeance for the man it killed, the meat the carcass will provide, and the entertainment of watching the shooting. "The people expected it of me and I had got to do it" (7), he writes. There is an implication that if he decided not to shoot the elephant, both he and the empire would suffer a loss of prestige, but the main concern in Orwell's mind is the "long struggle not to be laughed at" (7). He is even afraid to "test" the animal's mood by going closer for fear it might attack and kill him before he could shoot, thus giving the crowd a sight it would enjoy as much as the slaughter of the beast.

4. Despotic governments result from the need to maintain power over subtly resistant people. Such a government can rule only by fulfilling the people's expectations and responding to every crisis with the expected force. Orwell points to the irony that he stood armed in front of an unarmed crowd, yet he was powerless to do as he wished or as his judgment told him. Instead, he felt himself "an absurd puppet pushed to and fro by the will of those yellow faces behind" (7).

5. *imperialism* (2): a country's policy of gaining power by acquiring and ruling territories

    prostrate (2): lying face down, as in submission or adoration

    despotic (3): tyrannical, all-powerful

    mahout (3): the keeper and driver of an elephant

    miry (5): swampy, muddy

    conjurer (7): magician

    futility (7): uselessness, ineffectiveness

    sahib (7): "Master"; Indian title of respect when addressing Europeans

Questions About the Writer's Craft (p. 188)

1. What Orwell calls a "tiny incident" lasted only a short time, perhaps only an hour. Orwell uses clear transitions of time to keep us oriented as to what is happening, but he provides no specific clock time. "Early one morning," the narrative begins (3); after the death of the coolie, the action steps up, and the transitions indicate things are happening at a rapid pace: "he could not have been dead many minutes" (4); "As soon as I saw the dead man" (4); "The orderly came back in a few minutes" (5); "meanwhile some Burmans had arrived" (5); "As soon as I saw" (6); "I thought then" (6); "But at that moment" (7); "And suddenly I realized" (7); "And it was at this moment" (7); "I perceived in this moment" (7); "But I had got to act quickly" (8); "For at that moment" (9); "When I pulled the trigger" (11); "In that instant, in too short a time" (11); "He looked suddenly stricken" (11); "At last, after what seemed a long time—it might have been five seconds" (11); "And then down he came" (11). Orwell then describes the refusal of the animal to die: "I waited a long time"; "Finally I fired"; "but still he did not die" (12). The incident ends with Orwell leaving the scene but learning later that the animal took half an hour to die.

2. The first two paragraphs introduce us to the alien, far-off world where the narrative took place. In addition to setting the scene, Orwell explains what he was doing in Burma and, more importantly, gives us an emotional perspective from which to view the event. We learn in a general way about the bitterness between the colonialists and the native inhabitants and about the psychological effect his job as a policeman had on him. His confession that he was "young and ill-educated" and not even aware the British Empire was collapsing helps us feel empathy for him in the incident that follows. Without this information, we might not be willing to forgive him for shooting the elephant or for its horrible death or be able to comprehend the sense of victimization he felt despite his position as an "authority."

3. Orwell uses analogies in three important places. Two of the analogies are from the theater and relate to the sense of falseness that Orwell feels about his role in the colony. With the crowd watching him, he compares himself to "a conjurer about to perform a trick" with "the magic rifle." Then he helps us to understand his own psychological state at that moment by using another theater image: "Here was I . . . seemingly the lead actor of the piece; but in reality I was only an absurd puppet pushed to and fro by the will of those yellow faces . . ."; in the East, he says, the white man "becomes a sort of hollow, posing dummy. . . . He wears a mask, and his face grows to fit it" (7). Paragraph 10 continues this analogy, as Orwell describes the crowd breathing "a deep, low, happy sigh, as of people who see the theatre curtain go up at last." The third analogy compares the elephant to an elderly person; as he watches the beast in the rice paddy, he feels it has a "preoccupied grandmotherly air."

4. After he fires the first shot, he says the elephant "looked suddenly stricken, shrunken, immensely old. . . . His mouth slobbered. An enormous senility seemed to have settled upon him. One could have imagined him thousands of years old" (11). Orwell vividly evokes the suffering of the elephant by carefully observing the animal's movements after the shot. He notices the subtle but "terrible change" that came over it, in which "every line of his body had altered." The analogy with an old man helps structure his observation that the elephant seemed paralyzed, then sagged to his knees and slobbered. Other trenchant details include the image of the animal standing "weakly upright" again and the image of him toppling "like a huge rock," "his trunk reaching skywards like a tree and trumpeting once" (11). In paragraph 12, Orwell provides a graphic description of the beast's death agony. He reports firing over and over; into a picture that has so far been in black-and-white, he interjects colors. He remembers that the elephant's "mouth was wide open" so that "he could see far down into caverns of pale pink throat" and that "the thick blood welled out of him like red velvet." In this paragraph, too, we hear sounds: the "dreadful noise" and the "tortured gasps" that continued "steadily as the ticking of a clock."

SOMEONE'S MOTHER

Joan Murray

Questions for Close Reading (p. 191)

1. Murray's thesis emerges during the course of the narrative in her final action; it is not explicitly stated. Instead, she shares her inner conflict with the reader in paragraphs

68

24 and 28: Should Murray hand the elderly woman over to the town's police to make sure the woman gets home and thus betray the woman's infirmity to her son, or should she honor the woman's wishes to wait for further assistance from a neighbor so that she can get home without her son's knowing she had been lost? Murray decides to honor the woman's wishes. The implied thesis is that sometimes it is better to leave a person's dignity intact, even if this involves some risk, than to take an action for the person's own good when that action runs counter to a person's wishes and will strip her of her autonomy.

2. The external conflict in this essay is the conflict between Murray and the hitchhiker, who argue about where Murray should drop her off. The internal conflict is Murray's own indecision about whether to drive the elderly woman straight to the police so Murray can be certain she is physically safe or instead to let her off in town to be helped by a passerby who knows her, in which case Murray will not know whether the woman makes it safely home. This internal conflict is complicated by Murray's sorrow and guilt about her own mother, whom she and her brother recently moved into a nursing home.

3. By "Things were getting clearer" Murray means she is beginning to understand that the woman's unwillingness to be dropped off at the police station or her church arises from the woman's fear that she will be put in a nursing home when her son finds out she has gotten lost again. The elderly woman is not being deliberately difficult; instead she is trying to protect her independence.

4. Murray decides to let the woman off at the drugstore because she realizes that if she takes the woman to the police or other town authorities the woman's son will find out and will probably arrange for her to move to a nursing home where she can be supervised. Although Murray realizes this may eventually happen, she doesn't want to be the cause of its happening now. This decision allows her to compensate a little for the guilt she feels about her own mother's unhappiness at living in a nursing home instead of in her beloved family home.

5. *jaunty* (3): lively, sprightly
   beret (3): a cap with a tight headband and a full, flat top
   lilting (3): characterized by a rhythmic swing
   shoulder (12): the untraveled side of a roadway
   agitated (19): disturbed, excited
   azaleas (20): ornamental flowering shrubs; a type of rhododendron

Questions About the Writer's Craft (p. 192)

1. Although Murray states events in chronological order, she uses few time-order transitional expressions. Instead she keeps the reader oriented with transitions that use spatial cues to describe key aspects of her journey along Route 20. In paragraphs 1 and 2, she describes passing the hitchhiker and deciding to turn around and go back for her. In paragraph 3, Murray "drove back up the hill." In paragraph 12, Murray "glances down the road" and lists the businesses she sees. In paragraph 15, she and the hitchhiker are "on our way to Nassau," where the old woman lives. The journey continues in paragraph 24 with "as we drove" and ends in paragraph 25 with "When I pulled into the parking strip."

2. The descriptions of the elderly hitchhiker add vivid details to the essay, helping to bring the woman to life and to underscore both her vitality and her vulnerability. For example, in paragraphs 1 and 2, Murray describes the glimpse she caught of the hitchhiker as she drove by, "waving both arms"—a glimpse that made her turn back. In paragraph 3, Murray describes the woman close-up. Her clothing ("dark blue raincoat, jaunty black beret") and her appearance ("wisps of white hair lilting as the trucks whizzed by" and "the same broad grin") enable us to picture the woman as well as the setting at the side of the road. In paragraph 21, we learn that the woman has a "white dove pinned to her lapel," a detail that tells Murray she belongs to a church but that also tells us the woman still cares for her appearance.

3. Although the sections in which Murray tells her thoughts tend to slow the pace of the narrative, they are essential for expressing the tension between Murray's concern for the hitchhiker's safety and her concern for the woman's dignity and autonomy. These passages express this tension by recounting Murray's memories of her aging mother's decline and eventual institutionalization in a nursing home. Being privy to Murray's thoughts is necessary for the reader to understand the conflict at the heart of the essay and the thesis. Without them, there would be little evidence of internal conflict—the narrative would simply recount events.

4. The dialogue in this essay contributes to its realistic feel similarly to the way the descriptions of the hitchhiker contribute to a full and rich picture of events. It also helps advance the narrative, since much of the essay consists of the conversation Murray has with her passenger. In paragraphs 4–11, 13–19, and 21–28, we learn about what is happening through this conversation.

70

ANSWERS FOR CHAPTER 12
"ILLUSTRATION" (p. 195)

OPENING COMMENTS

When we first started teaching, we were caught off guard by students' seeming inability to provide detailed, specific examples in their papers. But we soon uncovered the reason for the vagueness of their writing. Many of them arrived in college with the notion that good writing is abstract and full of highfalutin language. Warned over and over not to pad their papers, many students had come to regard specific details and "for instances" as fluff.

We've found an almost surefire way to help students appreciate how powerfully examples can affect a reader. We have them react to two versions of some student writing, one enlivened with specifics, the other flat, lifeless, and sorely in need of supporting details. When we question students about their reactions ("Which version is more interesting? Which gives you more of a sense of the writer?"), we actually see them coming to grasp the full importance of vigorous supporting details.

Next we spend some class time on prewriting activities. This helps students learn how to generate examples for their essays.

That skill mastered, some of our eager-to-please students then give us too much of a good thing. They force readers to wade through a mass of specifics that don't add focus or drama to the essay's idea. When this happens, we emphasize that writers need to be selective and choose only the most striking, telling examples to support a point.

Varied in subject and mood, the professional selections in this chapter illustrate the power writing derives from rich supporting detail. By piling on instances of how preteens are encouraged to mature too soon, Hymowitz ("Tweens: Ten Going on Sixteen") provides a convincing case that the "tween" phenomenon has come to dominate youth culture. In "Bombs Bursting in Air," Johnson illustrates, through a series of poignant personal-experience examples, the precarious nature of the human condition. Finally, Wilson ("The Miracle of Melancholia") questions whether sadness can be a blessing in disguise as the author reflects on how sadness affected the lives and work of a number of artists.

ACTIVITIES: ILLUSTRATION

Below we provide possible responses to selected activities at the end of Chapter 12. Of course, your students are bound to come up with their own approaches.

Prewriting Activities (p. 210)

1. There are many ways to use illustration in these two essays; the lists below only begin to name the possibilities. We suggest that you have students share their ideas for examples, perhaps with a partner or in small groups. Seeing what others have come up with makes the point clearly that writing involves invention and individuality.

    Topic: Why public-school teachers quit

        Teacher who has to work a second job to support family
        Ex-teacher now a mail carrier, better paid
        Science teacher recruited by industry
        Teacher resenting blame and criticism of education today
        Teacher toiling late at night over tests and lesson plans

    Topic: Defining a preppy

        Female wearing pearls with baggy shorts on a chilly day
        Male wearing rugby striped shirt with a crest and loafers
        Preppies' conversation centering on grades and careers
        Preppie male going out for crew or tennis
        Preppie female playing intramural lacrosse or field hockey

Revising Activities (p. 211)

We suggest you offer students the chance to read each other's revised versions of the paragraphs in Activities 5, 6, and 7. Such exposure to others' work helps them to see new ways of handling the revision and can encourage them to be more creative.

5. Here are the main problems with the paragraph:

    — Needs examples of how stores might be modernized: new signs, more professional window display, interior renovation.

— Nature of the improvements to streets should be shown by examples: potted plants, outdoor sculptures, decorative benches, outdoor cafés.

— Examples needed of how town could be made more "fun to walk."

— Examples of the "attention-getting events" should be provided.

6. Here are some notes about the problems in the paragraph:

— "When we act foolishly or wildly" is general and self-evident.

— The "qualms" felt later are vague.

— The situation behind someone wanting "revenge" is obscure, making this detail unconvincing.

— What it is like to "feel bad" because of the superego's influence needs to be shown by illustration.

Here's the way an extended example might work in this paragraph:

The superego is the part of us that makes us feel guilty when we do something that we know is wrong. A young person might feel guilt after an evening of carrying on. For example, suppose a group of bored young men get "a fun idea" driving into town late one Saturday night. They buy cartons of eggs and bombard semi-conscious homeless men and haggard-looking prostitutes with raw eggs and unprintable names. Feeling superior, they laugh themselves silly. The next day, however, they might wake up depressed at the thought of their treatment of unfortunate human beings. Their superego is finally at work, making them recognize their own evil side. I can affirm the power of the superego, because in my senior year of high school I was involved in just such a caper.

7. It's a good idea to provide time in class for students to read over each other's revisions of this paragraph. Seeing how others handled the revision can give students a stronger sense of their revision options.

Here are the main problems with the paragraph:

— Vague descriptions ("trendy," "fine") need replacement by vigorous images. A strong example or two is needed here.

— Point about trendy clothes should be tied into the idea of the costliness.

— Singling out women is sexist; at the very least such a charge needs supporting examples. Indeed, more thought may well show that men are similarly vulnerable.

— Shampoo example should occur at the end of the paragraph, because the movement of the paragraph is from things that don't wear out to things that do wear out. Change the opening words of the sentence to fit it into its new location.

— "Slight changes" is vague; an example is necessary.

— Statement that men are "naive" and are "hoodwinked" is sexist and irrelevant; this point also needs to be more clearly tied into the point that the desire for the new is costly to the consumer.

TWEENS: TEN GOING ON SIXTEEN

Kay S. Hymowitz

Questions for Close Reading (p. 216)

1. Hymowitz doesn't directly state her thesis. Instead she quotes others stating it: "There is no such thing as preadolescence anymore. Kids are teenagers at ten" (paragraph 3); "There's a deep trend . . . toward kids getting older younger" (6); "The 12- to 14-year-olds of yesterday are the ten to 12s of today" (6).

2. Tweens like to think of themselves as sophisticated: "flirtatious, sexy, trendy, athletic, cool" (7). Girls project this image by wearing body adornment such as makeup or earrings, attention-getting hairdos, and trendy, often sexually suggestive clothes. Comparably, boys exemplify tweendom in an increased concern with fashion, especially pricey designer wear, as well as in other aspects of personal appearance, such as piercings and ultramodern hairstyles.

74

3. A growing number of children under the age of 15 are committing violent crimes (12); engaging in sexual activity (13–14); using alcohol and drugs, especially marijuana (15); and developing eating disorders (16).

4. She attributes the tween phenomenon primarily to parental absence and "a sexualized and glitzy" marketplace (18). These two factors, in turn, elevate the authority and influence of tweens' peer groups, resulting in a vicious circle of negative influences. Another cause that Hymowitz addresses but seems to regard as secondary is the earlier physical maturation of kids today than in the past (17).

5. *glowering* (1): staring with an angry look
   Talmudic (1): relating to a particular collection of ancient Jewish religious writings
   rites (1): religious ceremonial acts
   demographic (3): relating to population trends
   pragmatic (5): practical
   ideological (5): relating to a body of beliefs
   regalia (8): finery
   donning (8): putting on
   ply (8): participate in
   emblazoned (10): prominently marked
   de rigueur (10): required
   eschewing (11): rejecting
   tentative (14): hesitant
   proclivities (14): inclinations
   connotations (14): suggested meanings
   stigma (15): mark of disgrace
   pernicious (16): harmful
   correlation (17): co-occurrence, correspondence
   augment (18): increase

Questions About the Writer's Craft (p. 216)

1. The personal nature of this example draws the reader's interest, as do the variety of specific examples Hymowitz presents to illustrate her point. In addition, this anecdote gains Hymowitz credibility in discussing the topic of tweens, because it establishes her own personal experience with the phenomenon.

2. In addition to citing specific names (1, 8) and anecdotes (14), which reinforce the pervasive nature of the tweendom phenomenon, Hymowitz gives statements from a number of experts that bolster her view of the alarming behavior of tweens (3, 6–9, 13, 15–16). Moreover, she also cites statistics on the increase in crime by tweens (12), increased sexual activity and precocious physical maturity (13, 17), and tweens' drug use (15). The statistics are compelling, but the source materials are not always clearly stated. A "report by the Office of Juvenile Justice and Delinquency Prevention" is quoted about crime, but it would be hard for a reader to find the report. The statistic on drug use comes from *Raising Cain*, by Michael Thompson of the Harvard Medical School. But though the source seems reliable, there is no indication of how Thompson arrived at the information. For the statistics on sexuality, Hymowitz provides no source information at all. So while Hymowitz's use of statistics is very effective and persuasive, the reader could question her handling of source information, even given the less rigorous citation requirements for a nonacademic reading such as this one.

3. Hymowitz's tone is concerned and disapproving, somewhat bitter, and sometimes mocking or sarcastic. For example, she dismissively states that her daughter reads movie ads "with all the intensity of a Talmudic scholar" (1). Hymowitz renders the word "empowered" ironical by placing it in quotation marks (5) and sarcastically says that students "showed their respect" by dressing like prostitutes (8). Strongly negative terms such as *vulgar* (5), *crass* (5), *hooker* (9), *painted* (9), and *pernicious* (16) clearly convey Hymowitz's disapproval.

4. In these paragraphs, Hymowitz uses female clothing as a way of contrasting the preteens of earlier generations with today's tweens. She demonstrates the gap between the childish, modest clothing such as "little-girl flowers, ruffles, white socks, and Mary Janes" (8) worn in the past and the less-modest or sexually provocative clothing such as tank tops (discussed in paragraph 9), black minidresses (8), platform shoes (8), "midriff-revealing shirts" (8), and miniskirts (8) worn by comparably aged girls today.

BOMBS BURSTING IN AIR

Beth Johnson

Questions for Close Reading (p. 222)

1. The thesis is stated through a metaphor at the very end of the essay: "[Bombs] can blind us, like fireworks at the moment of explosion. . . . But if we have the courage to keep our eyes open and welcoming, even bombs finally fade against the vastness of the starry sky" (15). In other words, life's unexpected tragedies can seem devastating and insurmountable when they occur; but we must courageously live on, recognizing that even these misfortunes are part of life's greater mystery and beauty.

2. Johnson states directly, "News that reached me today makes me need to feel her [Maddie] near" (2), referring to the revelation that Maddie's 5-year-old playmate, Shannon, was unexpectedly diagnosed with a brain tumor. This jarring discovery reminds Johnson of the fragility of life and the randomness of misfortune, for Maddie could just as easily have been the one stricken with the tumor. Compelled by the maternal impulse to protect her child from impending harm, Johnson draws Maddie near. Though Johnson knows she has no power over the bombs that might explode in life, she feels slightly more secure having her daughter nearby.

3. The reactions of Maddie, Sam, and Johnson to the news of Shannon's illness provide a snapshot of the process of evolving maturity. Only 5 years old, Maddie fails to understand the gravity of Shannon's condition, and she is too young to be "faze[d]" by bombs in general (8). Johnson sees her younger self in Maddie, recalling her own "childhood . . . feeling of being cocooned within reassuring walls of security and order" (8). Maddie declares her certainty that Shannon "will be okay," having learned in school about a boy who recovered from an illness (5, 7). Maddie's confidence in Shannon's recovery and her willingness to change the subject—"Can we go to Dairy Queen?" (7)—contrast with the response of 13-year-old Sam, who is "not so easily distracted" (6). Perched between childhood and adulthood, Sam is aware of how serious Shannon's condition is, yet he still seeks his mother's guarantee that the child will recover: "She'll be okay, though, right?" (6). Just like his mother in her adolescence, Sam struggles as "the protective curtain between us and the bombs" (10) is slowly being drawn away from him. Finally, Johnson represents the adult stage of awareness, for she is most shaken by the news and is least confident that a happy ending is in sight. This essay itself serves as a testament to how much the news has affected her, for Shannon's "bomb" has inspired Johnson to reflect on life's

bombs in general. Having lived through numerous occasions when very bad things have happened to very good people, Johnson lacks any illusions about life's fairness. During Johnson's adolescence, the sudden death of her best friend taught Johnson the life-changing lesson that "there was no magic barrier separating me and my loved ones from the bombs. We were as vulnerable as everyone else" (11). Because the friend died in her sleep without contributing to her own demise in any way, Johnson as a teenager was forced to realize that no rules of logic or fairness govern the bursting of bombs. Nevertheless, as an adult, she demonstrates the need for comfort that characterizes children; she draws her child close to her and takes solace in the conclusion that despite the bombs that potentially may burst, life must be lived and people must be loved.

4. Given the knowledge that "the greater our investment in life, the larger the target we create" for life bombs, individuals may respond in one of two ways. One option is to withdraw from life and scale back commitments to others, reducing the potential for pain and loss. In Johnson's words, people may "refuse friendship, shrink from love, live in isolation, and thus create for ourselves a nearly impenetrable bomb shelter" (13). The other option is to immerse oneself in life, to be willing to brave potential bombs in order to experience life's joys and beauties, "to truly live, to love and be loved" (13). Johnson advocates the latter path, and she marvels at the resilience of the human spirit, which inspires people to live on: "I am moved by the courage with which most of us, ordinary folks, continue soldiering on. We fall in love, we bring our children into the world, we forge our friendships, we give our hearts, knowing with increasing certainty that we do so at our own risk" (13). Those who isolate themselves from life, she implies, lose far more in the end than those who say "yes, yes to life" and only periodically suffer.

5. *ferrying* (4): transporting
    shrapnel (6): fragments from exploded artillery
    faze (8): disturb; disconcert
    cocooned (8): sheltered; protected
    tremors (9): vibrations
    incantations (10): charms or spells ritually recited
    vulnerable (11): susceptible to harm or injury
    intertwining (12): joined together; interrelated
    impenetrable (13): unable to be entered or understood
    soldiering on (13): bravely moving forward
    prognosis (14): predicted outcome of a disease
    fragility (14): state of being breakable

Questions About the Writer's Craft (p. 222)

1. The first example that Johnson emphasizes—and the one that frames her essay—is the anecdote about Shannon. (Johnson ponders the sad news about Shannon's illness, then delivers the news to her children.) This incident receives so much attention for several reasons. It reminds Johnson of how fragile life is, how randomly calamity strikes, and, therefore, how easily one of her own children could have been the target of a "bomb" like the one that hit Shannon. This news then triggers a series of memories about tragedies that Johnson witnessed in the past and jars her into meditating on the occurrence of misfortune in general.

    These memories are ordered chronologically, beginning with incidents in Johnson's youth that affected her least and progressing to events in her adolescence and adulthood that impacted her most. In paragraph 9, she briefly catalogues "tiny shockwaves"—incidents that were peripheral to her life. She does not describe these memories in great detail, because, as she admits, she was unaware of the gravity of these incidents as a child and young adolescent. In paragraph 10, however, she says, "As we got older, the bombs dropped closer." She goes on to catalogue more harrowing events, ones that were closer to her life, such as a peer's suicide and the deaths of a carful of acquaintances. Yet, she says, "we still had some sense of a protective curtain between us and the bombs." But in paragraph 11, Johnson describes the single most destructive bomb, the one that changed her life. Here she develops at great length the example of her best friend's sudden death at the age of 16. She focuses on this crisis because of her degree of intimacy with this friend (as opposed to earlier acquaintances) and because this tragedy marked a turning point for Johnson, a rite of passage from innocent childhood into knowing maturity. After this event, she "found [herself] shaken to the core of [her] being" (11), more worldly-wise and less secure in the world around her. Johnson then quickly catalogues bombs that dropped in her late-adolescent and adult life. She does not focus special attention on them, because, as an adult, she was more equipped to handle the barrage of misfortune that she witnessed—secondhand, in one instance (her professor's loss of two children), and firsthand, in others (the pain of love, the failure of her marriage, and the death of her father). She says, "I became more aware of the intertwining threads of joy, pain, and occasional tragedy that weave through all our lives" (12); as a result, she came to regard misfortune as part of life's cycle and was not as rattled when it ran its course.

2. In paragraph 6, Johnson contrasts how she wishes life could be with how life actually is. She begins by describing a more ideal world, signaled by a series of sentences beginning with "I want." She wishes she could, in all honesty, assure her son that Shannon will be fine; that her children could "inhabit a world where five-year-olds

79

do not develop silent, mysterious growths in their brains" to begin with; that the medical terms being applied to Shannon were "words for *New York Times* crossword puzzles, not for little girls" (6). However, this fantasy is cut short by the blunt, bleak admission "But I can't," followed by her reason for abandoning illusions: "the bomb that exploded in Shannon's home has sent splinters of shrapnel into ours as well, and they cannot be ignored or lied away" (6). This stark contrast between wish and reality supports Johnson's main idea that in life we have no control over when and where bombs will drop: all we can do is live fully and love each other in order to weather life's inevitable misfortunes.

3. Johnson uses repetition in these two paragraphs, usually to emphasize magnitude and/or quantity. In paragraph 9, the similarly structured "*There was the* little girl who . . . ," "*There was the* big girl who . . . ," "*A* playful friendly custodian . . . ," and "*A* teacher's husband . . ." appear consecutively as Johnson itemizes the different people affected by bombs in her youth. The repetitive syntax emphasizes the number of bomb victims while also demonstrating how a wide range of people were equally vulnerable. Johnson employs repetition for the same reason at the beginning of paragraph 10, where she again itemizes bomb victims: "*A* friend's sister . . . ," "*A* boy I thought I knew . . . ," "*A* car full of senior boys . . . ." Later in the same paragraph, she reiterates "if only" four times to illustrate how she and her peers were powerless in the face of such tragedy, left only to repeat the same futile phrase over and over again.

4. The title, "Bombs Bursting in Air," introduces the central image of bombs, an image that reverberates throughout the essay. The title is derived from the line in "The Star-Spangled Banner" sung expressively by Johnson's daughter, Maddie, at the athletic event that opens the essay (2). Maddie's lively emphasis on the "b"s triggers a series of painful reflections for the author, who is still reeling from the devastating news about young Shannon's brain tumor. Johnson comes to refer to such unanticipated tragedies in life as "bombs," which burst in air—and in life—without warning and with lasting effect. She goes on in the essay to delineate the impact and aftermath of bombs in her own past, using terms like "exploded" (3), "shrapnel" (6), "shockwaves," and "tremors" (9) in showing how she grew out of youthful naïveté and into painful awareness of life's dark realities. The more one opens oneself up to life and love, she observes, "the larger the target" one becomes for devastation and loss (13). Despite her dark awareness, Johnson emerges with a renewed faith in the human spirit that inspires "ordinary folks [to] continue soldiering on" (13). At the end of the essay, she says that humans are faced with a choice: we may either withdraw from life in order to avoid potential bombs, or we may courageously "keep

our eyes open and welcoming," realizing that "even bombs finally fade against the vastness of the starry sky" (15).

Overall, the metaphor of bombs is effective not only because it captures the explosive impact that life's calamities may have but also because it is a highly accessible image for readers.

THE MIRACLE OF MELANCHOLIA

Eric G. Wilson

Questions for Close Reading (p. 226)

1. Wilson first states his thesis in paragraph 2: "A person can only become a fully formed human being, as opposed to a mere mind, through suffering and sorrow." He restates it with a somewhat different emphasis in paragraph 15, near the close of the essay: "We need sorrow, constant and robust, to make us human, alive, sensitive to the sweet rhythms of growth and decay, death and life."
2. Wilson believes that the "American addiction to happiness" leads to a "contented status quo" and "untapped possibilities" (15). It also causes Americans to try to increase happiness by taking "pills that reduce sadness, anxiety and fear" (3). As a result of an emphasis on happiness, according to Wilson, many Americans are shortchanging themselves of their full humanity.
3. Wilson's distinction between melancholia and depression is not clear. Instead, he suggests they are on a continuum. He puts depression, a mental illness that can lead to madness or suicide, at the extreme end of the continuum (16); in contrast, he does not characterize melancholia as an illness but indicates that it can lead to mental illness, as in O'Keeffe's case (12).
4. The title of the essay, "The Miracle of Melancholia," refers to the beautiful art that can emerge from an artist's suffering, as shown in the examples of Keats, Handel, O'Keeffe, and Mitchell. All of these artists suffered from melancholia, and many of their great works emerged after periods of suffering. In paragraph 9, Wilson indicates that the "metamorphosis of sadness to joy" is a perennial theme of Western art.
5. *affront* (3): insult
    delusion (4): a false belief
    bereft (5): deprived of the use or possession of something
    assiduously (6): with careful attention
    melancholia (9): a mental condition characterized by depression
    exuberance (9): joyous lack of restraint
    libretto (11): the text of a work for the opera or other musical theater

squalid (11): filthy and degraded
quelling (13): quieting, pacifying
status quo (15): the existing state of things
wantonly (16): without limitation or check
valorizing (17): enhancing, validating

Questions About the Writer's Craft (p. 226)

1. The single statistic, from the Pew Research Center, that "85% of the population claims ... to be 'very happy' or at least 'happy'" (2), provides a context for Wilson's essay and also supports an argument against his thesis. To counter this statistical example, Wilson relies on anecdotes about artists. He supports his thesis by describing the effects of melancholia on the art of John Keats, George Frideric Handel, Georgia O'Keeffe, and Joni Mitchell. His use of these examples is effective as far as it goes. However, by choosing only anecdotes about artists, he implies that the benefits of melancholia do not extend to the lives of ordinary people.

2. Wilson first uses Keats to introduce the essay and pose the question that the thesis answers. Keats poses this question in a letter to his brother, which Wilson quotes in paragraph 1: "Do you not see how necessary a World of Pains and troubles is to school an Intelligence and make it a Soul?" Wilson then resumes the Keats example, the first of four, in paragraph 6, narrating a summary of events that Keats suffered and claiming that his beautiful poetry emerged from this suffering.

3. This essay has a causal claim—that the experience of melancholia helps people to be fully human and alive. This claim is stated directly in paragraphs 2 and 15. In paragraphs 7, 8, and 9, Wilson uses the Keats example to show how creativity and "exuberance" arose from suffering and melancholia. He provides additional examples of suffering leading to artistic creation: Handel's masterpiece *Messiah* (10–11), O'Keeffe's landscape paintings (12–13), and Mitchell's claim that without the "demons" of melancholia the "angels" of art would disappear (14).

4. Students may have differing assessments about whether Wilson effectively addressed his audience, the readers of the Los Angeles *Times*. On the one hand, L.A. *Times* readers, like all human beings, can appreciate the universal emotions and experiences discussed in this essay, and in that sense this essay would appeal to readers of all kinds. Many L.A. *Times* readers are also well educated; thus they are familiar with the artists and the artwork that Wilson cites as supporting evidence for his thesis, and they are comfortable with his vocabulary, which is rather high-level. On the other hand, the L.A. *Times* probably has quite a few readers who are not familiar with the

artists that Wilson discusses and whose command of English vocabulary would be challenged by this essay. Since Wilson proves his thesis by using only artists as examples, this suggests that the "miracle of melancholia" may not happen to ordinary people—shutting out the majority of L.A. *Times* readers.

ANSWERS FOR CHAPTER 13
"DIVISION-CLASSIFICATION" (p. 230)

OPENING COMMENTS

We sometimes feel slightly uneasy about teaching division-classification as a distinct pattern of development. After all, the logic at its core comes into play often during the writing process. For example, when students generate and group ideas during the prewriting stage and when they outline their material, they necessarily draw on the ordering principles of division-classification. Even though many students can instinctively use it, we still teach division-classification as a discrete pattern of development. Understanding it helps students appreciate the demands of logical analysis.

We recommend covering division-classification early in the semester, although work on this pattern can be deferred. Students weak in analysis profit from an explicit discussion of the way to break down ideas and establish categories. And all students gain from analyzing essays to determine whether division and/or classification form the main organizational principle.

Working with division-classification can cause two problems for students. First, they sometimes become confused about the difference between division and classification. They think they're classifying when they're dividing and dividing when they're classifying. We state as succinctly as we can the difference between these two related but separate processes: Division involves taking a *single unit* or a *concept, breaking the unit down* into its *parts*, and *analyzing the connection* among the parts and between the parts and the whole. Classification *brings two or more related items together* and *categorizes* them according to type or kind.

Second, some students view division-classification as a pointless exercise designed by overly particular composition teachers. When they learn that they've been using division-classification all along (when brainstorming, when outlining, and so on), they begin to understand that division-classification is a valuable tool for logical analysis. In this regard, the student essay "The Truth About College Teachers" (pages 239–41) will provide the class with a good laugh (perhaps even at your expense) and help students see how to use classification to make a point.

This chapter's professional essays show how division-classification can help writers shed light upon a subject. McClintock ("Propaganda Techniques in Today's Advertising") uses division to demonstrate how American advertisers use propaganda to get us to buy their products. Sanders ("The Men We Carry in Our Minds") uses his classification of men as the basis for an essay in personal discovery. Winik ("What Are Friends For?") classifies the types of friendships we all have.

ACTIVITIES: DIVISION-CLASSIFICATION

Below we provide possible responses to selected activities at the end of Chapter 13. Of course, other approaches are possible.

Prewriting Activities (p. 244)

1. Division-classification can be used in a variety of ways in these two essays. Below are a few suggestions. It's a good idea to have students share their ideas on the use of division-classification with each other; this will provide a concrete demonstration of the possibilities.

    Topic: How to impress college instructors

    > Divide brownnosing techniques into types
    > Classify students according to their favorite technique
    > Classify instructors according to what impresses them

    Topic: Why volunteerism is on the rise

    > Divide to obtain motivations for volunteerism
    > Classify people needing help
    > Classify kinds of people who are apt to volunteer

2. Here are some possible principles of division for each of the topics. Other principles of division and theses are possible.

    a. **Prejudice**

    Principle of division: According to how prejudice develops
    Thesis: A prejudice against a group may be learned from one's parents, absorbed from society, or based on a bad experience of one's own.

    Principle of division: According to whether the prejudice is dangerous
    Thesis: Most of us have prejudices; some are trivial, such as a bias against broccoli; others are harmless, such as an intolerance for

85

whiners; still others are hurtful, such as a mistrust of a racial, ethnic, or religious group.

Principle of division: According to the motivation for the prejudice
Thesis: Prejudice against another group of people can be motivated by fear, jealousy, or ignorance.

b.   Pop Music

Principle of division: According to era
Thesis: Pop-music styles fall into distinct eras: music of the seventies, eighties, and nineties.

Principle of division: According to audience
Thesis: Pop music appeals to many audiences: the middle-aged, the yuppie, the college aged, and the teenage.

Principle of division: According to its origin
Thesis: Pop music has diverse influences: rock music, rhythm and blues, and hip-hop.

c.   A Shopping Mall

Principle of division: According to time of day at mall
Thesis: At different times of the day, different groups of people inhabit the mall: senior "mall walkers" in the early morning, business people grabbing lunch at midday, mothers and babies in the early afternoon, and teenagers in the early evening.

Principle of division: According to what is sold
Thesis: The types of stores that prosper at Garvey Mall tell much about today's consumer; the majority of shops sell apparel, quite a few sell audio- and videotapes, but only one sells books.

Principle of division: According to places people congregate
Thesis: The fountain, the fast-food arcade, and the movie-theater patio at Garvey Mall are all social spots but for different types of people.

d.   A Good Horror Movie

Principle of division: According to person being victimized
Thesis: In *Kennel Horror II*, the victim is either an unsuspecting innocent, a helpless poor person, or a law-enforcement officer.

Principle of division: According to attack location
Thesis: The victims in *Kennel Horror II* are attacked in their own homes, in pleasant public places, or in isolated rural areas.

Principle of division: According to film shots
Thesis: Director Logan Bettari uses extreme close-ups, rapid pans, and jarring cuts to increase the tension in *Kennel Horror II.*

3. Here are some possible principles of classification and thesis statements for this topic. Your students, of course, may come up with different ones.

   Topic: The effects of expanding the college enrollment

   Principle of classification: According to which groups the expansion would affect
   Thesis: Expanding the college enrollment would severely affect the student body, the faculty, and the local townspeople.

   Principle of classification: According to effects on various aspects of college life
   Thesis: Expanding the college enrollment would have serious economic, social, and academic effects.

   Principle of classification: According to consequences for various academic departments
   Thesis: Expanding the college's enrollment will minimally affect most departments, somewhat affect departments with popular majors, and seriously affect departments offering many required courses.

Revising Activities (p. 245)

4. The essay is based on a principle of division; "experience" is divided according to areas: employment, academic, social.

   The principle of division is applied incorrectly in the second point. Instead of being about an area of experience, this point focuses on "negative" experiences, a broad division that doesn't fit with the other areas. Second of all, the point refers only to "optimists," while all the other points refer to everyone.

   The problem can be remedied by eliminating the second point, since there are already three other solid points to be made in the essay.

5. Make time for your students to share their revisions with each other. Seeing the work of others helps students see all the possibilities in revising.

   This paragraph divides the concept of "play," using as a principle of division how much the child's peers are involved in the play. The paragraph's organization is based on the chronological appearance of the stages in the child's growth. The principle is applied consistently, but there are some problems in organization and in the support offered.

   Here are the specific problems with the paragraph:

   — The discussion of the first stage ("babies and toddlers") needs a specific example or two of "their own actions."

   — The fourth sentence, about elementary-children's play, is incorrectly located in the paragraph that discusses the play of preschool children. Delete this sentence.

   — The discussion of the second stage ("parallel play") could use an example of the "similar activities" the children engage in and how the children might "occasionally" interact. Note the specific examples provided for the third stage.

   — The last sentence is irrelevant and contradictory because no connection is made between the "special delight in physical activities" and the social aspect of children's play. In addition, the second part of the sentence contradicts the topic (first) sentence. This point must be more thought-out and more details should be added.

PROPAGANDA TECHNIQUES IN TODAY'S ADVERTISING

Ann McClintock

Questions for Close Reading (p. 251)

1. McClintock's thesis is located at the end of the first paragraph: "Advertisers lean heavily on propaganda to sell their products, whether the 'products' are a brand of toothpaste, a candidate for office, or a particular political viewpoint."

2. Propaganda is the "systematic effort to influence people's opinions, to win them over to a certain view or side" (2) in terms of product choices, political candidates, or social concerns. Many people associate propaganda solely with the subversive campaigns of foreign powers or with the spreading of outrageous lies to an unwitting, innocent populace. But actually propaganda is all around us; it is used by all the special interests that vie for our attention, our dollars, and our votes. American advertising is pervaded with propaganda in its attempt to sell us commercial products, and our political climate suffers from blizzard after blizzard of propaganda before each election.

3. Advertisers use "weasel words" to "stack the cards" and distort facts so that their products appear superior. Weasel words are words that say more than they mean and suggest more value than they actually denote. For example, an ad might say a shampoo "helps control dandruff," but we might understand this to mean that it cures dandruff (19).

4. Consumers should be aware of propaganda techniques so they can resist the appeal of ads that distort the truth or pull at our emotions. Only when we can separate the actual message and evaluate it for ourselves are we doing the hard work of clear thinking: "analyzing a claim, researching the facts, examining both sides of an issue, using logic to see the flaws in an argument" (23).

5. *seduced* (1): enticed, entranced; misled
   warmongers (5): people who attempt to start wars
   elite (17): an exclusive or privileged group

Questions About the Writer's Craft (p. 252)

1. The definition of *propaganda* informs us about the term's true meaning and also clears up misunderstandings about the extent to which average Americans are subjected to propaganda. The broader purpose of providing us with this definition is to persuade us that advertising is indeed propaganda. McClintock hopes to motivate us to learn more about the various techniques of propaganda so we can protect ourselves from its daily onslaughts.

2. "Seduced" and "brainwashed" are both words with strong negative connotations; we are likely to be shocked or disbelieving when we read that "Americans, adults and children alike, are being seduced. They are being brainwashed" (1). By using these terms, McClintock challenges our belief in our independence and free will. Through the use of these and other terms ("victims"), she provokes us to continue reading the essay. Ironically, this use of loaded words manipulates the reader's reactions in a manner similar to that of propaganda.

3. Questions appear in the discussions of "Glittering Generalities" and "Card Stacking" and in the conclusion to the essay. In both the sections on propaganda techniques, the questions are rhetorical, in that they need no answers. They are questions used to make a point. For example, McClintock asks, "After all, how can anyone oppose 'truth, justice, and the American way'?" (6). The implied answer is, "No one can." In her discussion of specific empty phrases, the author asks questions to point out the meaninglessness of such statements as "He cares . . ." and "Vote for Progress" (7). These questions are meant not to be answered but to show the vagueness of glittering generalities. In the section on card stacking (18–20), she suggests that readers ask questions to test the validity of a political accusation such as "my opponent has changed his mind five times. . . ." The questions in the essay's conclusion, however, are real questions to which she provides answers.

4. Tied to McClintock's explanation of why propaganda works is a warning: To remain blind to the power of propaganda is to consent "to handing over our independence, our decision-making ability, and our brains to the advertisers" (24). In order to prevent this fate, McClintock advises us to do the work that clear thinking requires. This ending is an example of a call-for-action conclusion.

THE MEN WE CARRY IN OUR MINDS

Scott Russell Sanders

Questions for Close Reading (p. 256)

1. Sanders implies his thesis, which might be stated as, "People's early experiences of men's and women's roles determine their definitions of what it is to be a man and what it is to be a woman." In the first paragraph, the last sentence ("they [black convicts and white guards] have also come to stand for the twin poles of my early vision of manhood—the brute toiling animal and the boss") may seem to be the thesis, but the essay goes on to discuss more than just two categories of men. This statement about the "twin poles of my early vision of manhood" is the first of several statements that point out the types of men Sanders encountered in his youth. These initial two, the toiler and the boss, appear to be the first categories he recognized. Other categories are mentioned in paragraphs 4, 5, 6, and 10.

2. In his childhood, Sanders primarily encountered men who toiled, "men who labored with their bodies." The visible damage these men suffered included injured and scarred hands, squinty eyes, leathery faces. Internally they suffered bad backs, hernias, ulcers, achy knees and ankles, partial deafness, and clogged lungs (3). In addition to these "twisted and maimed" bodies, the men also seem to suffer spiritually. They smoked and drank (3), and their eyes looked "bruised." They grew old faster than the women. They clearly felt overworked, and the images of imprisonment and of their looking "as though somebody had been whipping them" convey a desperation of the soul.

3. There were a few non-laborers among the men Sanders knew as a child: male teachers, for example. He also came to know of various male professions from reading books and from watching television. But to him the professionals he saw on television—"the politicians, the astronauts, the generals, the savvy lawyers, the philosophical doctors, the bosses"—were too far away, too remote, to be believable. Such men were like "the figures in tapestries," artwork of another time and place. Although he perceived such professionals as "cool, potent creatures," he could not imagine ever becoming one.

4. The men Sanders knew in his youth had it much harder than the women; men suffered from their daily labor and died younger (2–3). When women he met in

91

college criticized men for harboring all the privilege and power, he "was baffled." The men he knew had no privilege and no power, only "maimed, dismal lives" (7). In fact, to his mind, women had easier lives, more flexible schedules, and less responsibility for the big issues of money and war. The pain women suffered from "men's bullying" was invisible to him because it had never been discussed (8). The college women carried different images of men than he did, because they came from backgrounds in which men were professionals, "the big wheels of the big cities" (10). These men "ran the world" (10).

5. *sodden* (1): soaked with liquid or moisture
    acrid (1): sharp and biting to the taste or smell
    marginal (2): bordering, on the edge of
    tapestries (5): heavy decorative woven fabrics with pictorial designs
    potent (5): possessing great controlling or ruling power
    grievances (8): resentments or complaints against unjust acts
    expansiveness (8): openness, lack of restraint
    tedium (9): the quality or state of being boring or monotonous

Questions About the Writer's Craft (p. 256)

1. Sanders describes the toilers and the warriors in the most detail. Paragraphs 1–3 discuss the laboring men, and he returns to them again in paragraphs 7 and 9 to add even further details. Although he describes soldiers in only one paragraph, 4, the powerful evocative images of their despair compose a weighty description of this type of male. His discussion of bosses is scattered through the essay and mainly provides generalities about this type of man. He sketches one type of boss briefly in paragraph 1 (the overseers), mentions his own father's white-collar job in paragraph 6, and makes some general observations about professionals in paragraph 10. The result is that we are given a more compelling image of the workingmen than of the bosses. We can feel what it was like to live and struggle as a laborer, but we get only images from afar of the professional class. Since Sanders did not experience the day-to-day lives of professionals, we might expect him to provide less information about them.

2. Sanders uses parallel structure and repetition to add drama and tension to his description of laborers' lives. In paragraph 2, most of the independent clauses begin with "they": "They were marginal farmers . . .," "they swept floors . . .," "they trained horses . . . .," "They got up before light . . .," "they worked on their own places. . . ." Within these sentences, Sanders piles up images by repeating grammatical forms. The men "were marginal farmers, . . . welders, steelworkers,

92

carpenters," he writes, repeating a series of nouns. From here on, he uses specific, action-revealing verbs to indicate the fierce work men did. "They swept floors, dug ditches, mined coal, or drove trucks . . ."; "they trained horses, stoked furnaces, built fires, stood on assembly lines. . . ."; "They got up before light, worked all day long. . . ."; "They worked on their own places. . . ." Then Sanders moves to a series of participles: "tilling gardens . . . fixing broken-down cars, hammering on houses. . . ."

In paragraph 3, Sanders uses a balance of adjectives to lend dignity to the horror of workingmen's lives. His first sentence here contains two pairs of balanced adjectives: "The bodies of the men I knew were *twisted* and *maimed* in ways *visible* and *invisible*." The second sentence continues this balancing, then breaks away from it dramatically in two short clauses: "The nails of their hands were *black* and *split*, the hands tattooed with scars. Some had lost fingers." The next sentence continues the balancing, here of adjectival phrases: "finicky backs and guts weak from hernias." The structure of this sentence, "*Heavy lifting had given them* . . .," is repeated in the next: "*Racing conveyor belts had given them* ulcers." From this point in paragraph 3, he begins to qualify the victims of the injuries: "Anyone who had worked for long around machines was hard of hearing. . . . Most of them coughed, . . . and most of them drank." Although less prominent, there are still some balanced and repeated phrases in this part of the paragraph: "*Most of them coughed*, from *dust* or *cigarettes*, and *most of them drank cheap wine* or *whiskey*, so their eyes looked *bloodshot* and *bruised*." The number of details and the balanced and even-paced way they are embedded in the sentences convey the flavor of the work the men endured. The reader gets a feeling of inevitability and relentlessness about the men's lives, and their circumstances seem unremittingly cruel and brutalizing. The impression is driven home at the end of paragraph 3, when Sanders notes dispassionately, "Men wore out sooner. Only women lived to old age."

3. The details Sanders provides about the lives of workingwomen and upper-class men serve, by contrast, to emphasize and dramatize the pain endured by workingmen. Confronted with the feminist point of view while at college, Sanders explains that his childhood indicated to him that women, not men, led the easier life. He then catalogues, point by point, how women seemed to have less stress, pain, and humiliation built into their roles. In paragraph 8, he mentions women's fostering of culture as a unique attribute that was lacking in men. Then he points out several areas of life in which men had it comparatively harder than women: being responsible for an income, having to wage war, and living an "ironclad," scheduled life. He concedes that there were some elements of women's suffering that he missed: for example, the lowly jobs held by women who did work and the physical abuse that some women secretly suffered. Ultimately, he compares working on an assembly line to caring for

a baby and concludes that the traditionally "female" job of child rearing is by far preferable.

In paragraph 10, Sanders describes the lives of professional men, the fathers of feminist college women, establishing an implicit contrast with the lives of workingmen. He points out that these men "drove cars that cost more than any of my childhood houses" (10). And, unlike the workers, "they were never laid off, never short of cash at month's end, never lined up for welfare." These details serve to underline one of Sanders's main points: that workingmen's lives are filled with struggle, failure, and despair.

4. Paragraph 7 is concerned with the author's confusion when he encountered college women who considered men privileged and selfish. Such an image of men did not connect with his own experiences of what men's lives were like. The questions show him attempting to interrogate his life and the men he knew in order to see if perhaps the women were on to something. He begins, "What privileges? What joys?" As he continues to ask questions, the wording reveals his answers. These are uniformly negative: he doesn't find the feminists' arguments at all applicable to the men in his past. He asks, "What had they stolen from their wives and daughters? The right to go five days a week, twelve months a year, for thirty or forty years . . .? The right to drop bombs and die in war? The right to feel every leak in the roof, every gap . . . every cough . . . as a wound they must mend? The right to feel, when the layoff comes or plant shuts down, not only afraid but ashamed?" The questions, with their strongly implied answers, become part of the author's argument that workingmen lead lives of pain and struggle.

WHAT ARE FRIENDS FOR?

Marion Winik

Questions for Close Reading (p. 260)

1. Winik states her thesis that "everybody can't be everything to each other, but some people can be something to each other" in the first sentence.
2. Winik divides her friends into eight categories: Buddies, Relative Friends, Work Friends, Faraway Friends, Former Friends, Friends You Love to Hate, Hero Friends, and New Friends. She seems to value Buddies, "the workhorses of the friendship world" (paragraph 2), Faraway Friends, who know you so well that they are

94

"indispensable" (8), and New Friends, whose novelty makes you interesting and whose friendship is "almost like falling in love" (15).

3. A Relative Friend differs from other relatives in that he or she shares your view of the family (3). Furthermore, while relationships with relatives are often "tinged with guilt and obligation, a relationship with a Relative Friend is relatively worry-free" (4).

4. The types of friends characterized by negative qualities include Former Friends, who are no longer friends because of some conflict or problem in the past (10); Friends You Love to Hate, who are inconvenient, awkward, and embarrassing (11); and, to a lesser extent, Hero Friends, whose lives are so good and useful that you can't live up to them (13).

5. *innumerable* (2): countless, very many
   tinged (4): affected or modified
   infallible (6): certain, unerring
   accentuate (6): emphasize
   wistful (10): musingly sad
   inopportune (11): inconvenient
   tonic (14): something that refreshes

Questions About the Writer's Craft (p. 260)

1. Winik divides her friends according to the benefits they confer on her. She makes them stand out sharply by naming and capitalizing each type of friend, which suggests that each is an archetype.

2. Besides division-classification, the main patterns are definition and exemplification. For each type of friend, Winik defines its essential characteristics. For example, the definition of a Hero Friend begins "These people are better than the rest of us" and continues until we understand the type (paragraph 13). Winik uses exemplification throughout the essay to help describe the function of each type of friend. For example, in regard to Buddies, Winik says, "They feed your cat when you are out of town and pick you up from the airport when you get back" (2). In regard to Faraway Friends, they help you remember the past, like "the name of your seventh-grade history teacher" (9).

3. The tone of this essay is mostly light with some occasional wistfulness. The capitalized names of each type of friend, the descriptions of each category, and the specific examples are often humorous. In addition, lightness and lack of seriousness result in part from the analysis of friends in purely selfish terms, as they relate to

Winik. Occasionally there is a wistful note, as in the description of Work Friends (6) and Former Friends (10).

4. Winik's title is effective because it states her principle of division—she will sort her friends into categories that reflect their usefulness to her. The essay does fulfill the expectations raised by the title, since Winik catalogs her friends by their functions in her life.

ANSWERS FOR CHAPTER 14
"PROCESS ANALYSIS" (p. 264)

OPENING COMMENTS

Like many of our colleagues, we cover process analysis early in the semester. This pattern of development teaches students a great deal about selectivity ("Which steps should I cover?" "How many examples should I provide?"), organization, and transition signals. Process analysis also highlights the importance of audience analysis. To explain the steps in a process clearly, the writer must identify what readers need to know and understand.

Students often expect process analysis to write itself; they expect it to unfold naturally and automatically. But once they get feedback on their first draft, they realize that the sequence of steps was self-evident only to them and that they need to work harder to make the process accessible to their readers.

This chapter includes process analysis that varies widely in subject. You may want to start with Stoll's "Cyberschool," which provides a tongue-in-cheek how-to for computerizing—and dehumanizing—America's schools. Also included here is Sutherland's "What Shamu Taught Me About a Happy Marriage," in which the author rids her husband of some annoying habits using animal-training techniques, and David Shipley's "Talk About Editing," which gives readers insight into the step-by-step editing process followed at a major U.S. newspaper.

ACTIVITIES: PROCESS ANALYSIS

Below we provide possible responses to selected activities at the end of Chapter 14. Of course, your students are bound to come up with their own approaches.

Prewriting Activities (p. 279)

1. Process analysis lends itself to these essay topics in several ways. Below are some possibilities. In class, we suggest you have students share their responses. They will be delighted to discover that their neighbors have devised different uses for process analysis in these essays.

    Topic: Defining comparison shopping

    > How a person might use a consumer magazine to compare the quality of DVD players
    > How a person might compare sneakers at a mall
    > How someone might call up car dealers to get the best price

    Topic: Contrasting two teaching styles

    > How two teachers respond to student questions
    > How two teachers deal with students who don't understand
    > How two teachers convey complex information

2. Many students will find a way to treat each topic both directionally and informationally, and you'll need to sort out in class what the most likely approaches would be in terms of a particular audience.

    a. Going on a job interview: Primarily directional, possibly informational, or both

    b. Using a computer in the library: Directional

    c. Cleaning up oil spills: Informational

    d. Negotiating personal conflicts: Primarily directional, possibly informational, or both

    e. Curing a cold: Directional, informational, or both

    f. Growing vegetables organically: Primarily informational, possibly directional, or both

Revising Activities (p. 280)

6. Encourage students to work together on this activity or have them share their revisions. Other students' responses will help them discover weaknesses in the paragraph they might otherwise overlook.

   Here are the main problems with the paragraph:

   — The chronology is disorganized. The second and third sentences, about keeping customers on the phone, should come later in the paragraph, after the opening of the phone call is discussed.

   — How one performs the steps in the process of making such a call is left vague. More details are needed to explain such aspects of the process as "setting the right tone," "in a friendly way . . . keep[ing] the prospective customer on the phone," "determin[ing]—in a genial way—why the person is reluctant to buy," "encourag[ing] credit card payment," and "end[ing] . . . in an easy, personable way."

   — The sentences discussing the loneliness of the typical person are a digression. The two sentences from "Maintaining such a connection . . ." through "a sad fact of contemporary life" should be deleted.

   — Throughout the paragraph, the caller is variously referred to as "you" and as "the salesperson." This shift in person should be corrected by choosing one or the other and sticking to it. The third person ("salesperson") may be more appropriate since few readers will be telephone solicitors.

7. We suggest you offer your students the chance to read each other's revisions of this paragraph. Exposure to other versions helps them see many more possibilities in revising.

   Here are the main problems in the paragraph:

   — To preserve the paragraph's chronology, the sixth sentence (beginning "Before heading to class . . .") and the seventh should come earlier in the paragraph. These two sentences should be placed after "lessen the trauma."

99

— Throughout the paragraph, there's a shift in person; for instance, "they" is used in the second sentence, but the third sentence shifts to "you"; it goes back and forth from there. The writer should choose one or the other and stick to it.

— The tenth and eleventh sentences, running from "A friend of mine . . ." to "volunteers to participate" are irrelevant and should be deleted.

— The point that you should "never, ever volunteer to answer" should be moved up to occur immediately after the advice about where to sit in sentences 8 and 9.

— The transition, "however" (sentence 12), doesn't work when the paragraph is reorganized as described above. A transition such as "also" would work well.

— The last two sentences, though in keeping with the paragraph's light tone, nevertheless seem a bit jarring. Furthermore, since they don't develop the essay's overall point, they probably should be eliminated.

CYBERSCHOOL

Clifford Stoll

Questions for Close Reading (p. 284)

1. Though Stoll's position is evident from the outset (when he refers to the "pessimal view of the schoolroom of the future"), he doesn't express his thesis until the ironic close of the essay's final paragraph: "Yep, jut sign up for the future: the parent-pleasin', tax-savin', interactive-educatin', child-centerin' Cyberschool. . . . No learning. Coming soon to a school district near you." Students may wish to refine this statement using their own words. Here is one possibility: "Though the computerization of the classroom seems to be inevitable, this trend will result in disastrous educational consequences for the students subjected to it."

2. The process of fully computerizing schoolrooms—or creating a "cyberschool"—is as follows: First, the school district buys a computer for every student (5) as well as educational software that matches the curriculum (6). This software will be customized to students' educational levels and personal tastes but most importantly to the standardized tests students are required to take (7–8). The computers will track students' progress and convey this information to parents and administrators (9).

Classroom desks will be replaced by cubicle workstations, essentially eliminating all student contact (11). Teachers and librarians will be fired or retrained as data-entry clerks and replaced by computer specialists and security guards (11–12). "Luxuries" such as art class and field trips will be eliminated to save money, while new profits can be derived from arranging corporate sponsorship of the cyberschool (14). Online extracurricular activities will allow students to "experience" community service and "interact" with people from around the world (18). As a result, test scores will rise dramatically, while costs decrease (13).

As is made apparent throughout by Stoll's sarcastic phrases, such as "Yee-ha!" (1) and "naw" (4), he opposes the overreliance on computers in the classroom. Overall, Stoll's dismissive yet cuttingly ironic attitude toward his subject is summarized in the sentence, "Yep, just sign up for the future: the parent-pleasin', tax-savin', teacher-firin', interactive-educatin', child-centerin' Cyberschool" (18).

3. In paragraph 3, Stoll points the finger at "harried" school-board members and other administrators, especially elected ones. These individuals are pressured to reduce educational costs while improving students' performance and placating taxpayers. In the minds of these individuals, Stoll asserts, the cyberschool model of education presents numerous benefits. First, the computerized classroom allows long-term reduction in education spending achieved through the firing of full-time teachers (3, 11, 12, 15) as well as the possibility of future profit through teaming with corporate supporters (14). Proponents also believe computers will allow students more customized learning, especially with regard to standardized-test preparation (6–8). They could facilitate instant feedback and surveillance of students' progress to parents and administrators (9, 18) while reducing contact—troublesome and otherwise—among students (10). In the eyes of proponents, computers could even be seen as fostering healthy extracurricular activities such as distance mentoring or international student buddying (17)—all vicariously through the computer and never through firsthand contact.

4. According to Stoll's characterization of the cyberschool, teachers will play little to no role. As he says, tongue in cheek, in paragraph 11, "Teachers are an unnecessary appendix at this cyberschool." Rendered "irrelevant" by the new multimedia-computer capabilities (11), by a "cadre of instructional specialists, consultants, and hall monitors" (12), and by "real-time instructors" available through "distance learning displays" (15), teachers and librarians will be "laid-off" and some can be "retrained as data entry clerks" (10).

Stoll's attitude, though tongue-in-cheek, also carries ominous overtones regarding the dehumanization of children's education. This becomes especially apparent in his vision of a Big Brother-esque online instructor available only via "distance learning displays" and "two-way video" (15). Similarly alarming is the idea of the school board's monitoring of everything that students learn "without idiosyncratic teachers to raise unpopular topics or challenge accepted beliefs" (16)—when in fact teachers' fostering of independent thinking among students is what many people value as essential to a good education. Stoll also seems to mock the idea of teachers being replaced by "instructional specialists, consultants, and security guards" (12), as if those functions are the only ones that teachers fill in children's lives.

5. *infrastructures* (1): underlying foundations, especially for an organization or system
   optimal (1): most favorable or desirable
   harried (3): distressed by repeated attacks or harassment
   placate (4): appease; allay the anger of, especially by making concessions
   adept (8): very skilled
   standardized (8): conforming to a standard
   cubicles (10): small compartments for work or study
   compartmentalized (10): separated into distinct parts
   cadre (12): small, tight-knit group of trained personnel
   recoup (14): return as an equivalent for; reimburse
   idiosyncratic (16): having a behavioral characteristic peculiar to an individual or group

Questions About the Writer's Craft (p. 285)

1. This is a "trick question" of sorts, given the irony at the heart of Stoll's essay. On its surface, the process being described could seem directional in nature, laying out the procedure for implementing the cyberschool model of education. Stoll goes into relative detail regarding the setup and administration of the cyberclassroom as well as the implications of doing so. The speaker of the essay, in all his ostensible enthusiasm for the cyberschool, almost provides a handbook to interested parties. But on closer look, it becomes apparent that this process analysis is, in fact, informational, primarily because Stoll presents the mechanics of a cyberschool in order to actually advocate *against* its implementation. He does so by offhandedly presenting the cyberschool's serious flaws and defects as though they are benefits; these include the reduction of precious interaction among teachers and students, elimination of independent or creative thinking, concentration solely on learning content of standardized tests, and so on.

2. Stoll's tone is dismissive and definitely ironic. In presenting the cyberschool, Stoll adopts a persona much like the voice in an infomercial—synthetic, hyper, and ultimately trying to sell junk. However, Stoll's actual cynical agenda comes through in much of the wording that disrupts the pro-cyberschool façade. The phrase "whatever that means" blows the cover on the self-important techspeak of paragraph 1, as do the artificially enthusiastic "Yee-ha!" (1) and "Naw—it's easy to solve all these problems" (4). The words "edutainment" (6) and "edu-games" (8) that Stoll coins reveal a cynical view of the education trends he challenges, implying their watered-down nature. This is reinforced by the image of a "chatty pony" or "Fred the Firefighter" assuming the instructional role that trained professional teachers currently occupy—an absurd and demeaning image. In fact, regarding teachers in the cyberschool, he says "No need for 'em" (11), a phrase that's obviously suspect in its flippancy. And the phrase "Virtual Compassion Corps" (17) is bursting with bitter contradiction, as is the statement, "All without ever having to shake hands with a real person . . . or (gasp!) face the real problems of another culture" (17). Overall, Stoll's dismissive yet cuttingly ironic attitude toward his subject is summarized in the sentence, "Yep, just sign up for the future: the parent-pleasin', tax-savin', teacher-firin', interactive-educatin', child-centerin' Cyberschool" (18). By referring to educational computers and their supporters in such dismissive terms, Stoll diminishes the stature of computers as a viable vehicle for teaching children, and he reinforces the central idea that computers are flashy distractions from the serious work of learning. The gravity of his message is resoundingly conveyed in the simple phrase "No learning."

   Regarding the effect of Stoll's tone on his overall message, students' answers may vary, though it is likely that many will argue his apparent flippancy and humor in handling the topic helps capture readers' attention and send home his point more effectively than a straightforward, dry argument would.

3. Based on the information conveyed about Stoll, he appears to have airtight credibility in writing on the topic of computers and their effect on children's education. As an astronomer and programmer of computers "since the mid-sixties," Stoll has both an intimate working knowledge of computers and a highly informed long-term perspective on their effects on society; this expertise indicates that he is a well-reasoned and well-intentioned computer user, not a fanatical technophobe. As a teacher of children and young adults, he has accumulated firsthand observations of the increasing emphasis on computers in the classroom and the effects of this emphasis on young people. Finally, as a father, he has likely seen the impact of computers on the various facets of children's lives as they grow. His passionate desire to stave off the crippling effects on children of computer overuse is therefore legitimized by his roles as scientist, teacher, parent—and avid computer user.

4. In paragraph 15, Stoll addresses the central argument against the computerization of education when he says, "Concerned that such a system might be dehumanizing? Not to worry." His speaker then goes on to present a series of quasi-human interactions—all involving computers—to "allay" the fear of mechanized learning. These include "interactive chat sessions" among kids (instead of conversation, play, or in-person group work), help from a "trained support mentor" via Internet (rather than a trained in-person teacher), and, if necessary, assistance from a real-time instructor via "distance learning display" and "two-way video" (and certainly not in person). Clearly, these examples—all of which demonstrate complete reliance on computers rather than human contact—offer little to no comfort regarding the concern that computerized classrooms will result in dehumanized education for children. For as long as computers are the sole conduit of communication between individuals, the charge of dehumanization will remain valid. Stoll has deliberately selected these examples to sabotage the counterargument because, in fact, his essay seeks to undermine the idea of the cyberschool.

WHAT SHAMU TAUGHT ME ABOUT A HAPPY MARRIAGE

Amy Sutherland

Questions for Close Reading (p. 290)

1. Sutherland's thesis emerges gradually. She begins with a narrative about ignoring her husband's irritated search for his keys (paragraphs 1–3). She then explains that she wanted to improve her husband but went about this the wrong way—through nagging and marriage counseling (6–8). Then, by observing animal trainers, she realizes that "the same techniques might work on that stubborn but lovable species, the American husband" (10). Finally, in paragraph 11, Sutherland states: "The central lesson I learned from exotic animal trainers is that I should reward behavior I like and ignore behavior I don't."

2. Sutherland first tries to change her husband's behavior by nagging, "which only made his behavior worse" (7), and then by going to a marriage counselor, who thought their marriage was fine (8). Sutherland then gives up on improving her husband until she encounters the animal trainers.

3. One technique that Sutherland tries is to ignore bad behavior, as she does in the introductory paragraphs and paragraph 22, where she describes Scott angrily searching for his keys. She also rewards good behavior; for example, she thanks Scott for putting a dirty shirt in the hamper (12). By using approximations, she rewards each small step toward learning a whole new behavior, thanking him and praising him for each little positive thing he does. Another approach Sutherland takes is to analyze her husband as an animal trainer analyzes a species. She decides Scott is a loner, an alpha male, balanced but slow, not punctual, and motivated by food (15). This analysis enables her to tailor her training to her husband's needs. For example, she uses the technique of "incompatible behaviors" to get Scott to leave her some space while she is cooking, by giving him food preparation chores to do on the other side of the kitchen (19).

4. By treating her husband as an exotic species of animal, Sutherland succeeds in modifying his behavior so that he is neater, less forgetful, and more helpful in the kitchen. All of these improvements result in a happier marriage because Sutherland finds him less irritating and he himself is calmer—there are fewer sources of conflict. Sutherland also accepts that there are some things about Scott that she cannot change, which means that she no longer gets frustrated by his inability to change them.

5. *bromides* (2): commonplace or hackneyed statements
   angst (2): a feeling of anxiety or apprehension
   mercurial (5): having fast, unpredictable changes in mood
   reeking (7): having a strong or offensive smell
   pirouette (9): a full turn on the ball of the foot or the toe
   basked (12): took pleasure in
   hierarchy (14): the classification of a group into rankings
   alpha male (15): a dominant male animal
   omnivore (15): an animal that eats both animals and plants
   emu (16): an Australian bird similar to an ostrich
   incompatible (17): incapable of co-existence
   provokes (20): provides a stimulus for
   affront (26): insult
   inadvertently (27): unintentionally
   tirade (30): an angry, lengthy speech

Questions About the Writer's Craft (p. 290)

1. Sutherland uses informational process-analysis in this essay. By using the first person, she communicates authoritatively, explaining how she trained her husband so

105

that he would be easier to live with by using techniques adapted from animal trainers. Her successful experience lends weight to the processes she is describing.

2. The tone of this essay is humorous. It's clear that Sutherland loves her husband, and so we can be amused at her application of animal-training techniques to his behavior. As she takes notes on the exotic animal species being trained, she's actually thinking of ways to apply what she's learning to training her husband (paragraphs 16, 21). When Scott responds well to one of her behavior-modification techniques, Sutherland says, "I felt as if I should throw him a mackerel" (22).

3. The other main pattern of development is narrative. The essay is organized like a story—the story of how Sutherland applies animal-training techniques to her husband, succeeds in improving his behavior, and finally becomes the subject of the techniques herself. Exemplification is also used in the essay, but it's not an organizing principle.

4. The conclusion of the essay is effective, because at the end Scott takes the techniques that Sutherland has used on him and begins to use them on her. Until that point, Sutherland had been doing a lot of manipulating, and some readers might find that unappealing, even though her husband took her actions with good humor. This turnabout helps balance their relationship from the reader's perspective. It also provides a neat narrative frame for the piece.

TALK ABOUT EDITING

David Shipley

Questions for Close Reading (p. 294)

1. Shipley states his thesis in paragraphs 2–4: The purpose of editing op-ed articles is to make sure that they are factually accurate and that the writer's argument is clear and sound. In paragraphs 2 and 3, he outlines the editing done to op-ed pieces and the collaboration with the author to finalize the copy. Finally, in paragraph 4, he states that the best way to explain op-ed editing is to walk through the process.

2. New York *Times* op-ed editors check grammar, correct typographical errors, make changes according to the newspaper's stylebook, check the article's length, fact-check, check assertions, and improve readability (8–17). Shipley devotes the most

space to explaining the process involved in checking assertions (four paragraphs) and improving readability (two paragraphs).

3. The relationship between the editor and the writer is a partnership, according to Shipley. Thus the writer gets to see and respond to all the changes that the editor has made or suggested, and nothing is published unless the writer and editor have agreed on all the necessary changes. Shipley focuses on the collaborative nature of this give-and-take; in paragraph 19, he emphasizes this by saying that, "Editing is not bullying." However, he also acknowledges that there can be conflict between editor and writer during this process (20).

4. By "Editing is a human enterprise," Shipley acknowledges that much editing is subjective. Editors may misunderstand a writer's point, may overlook a mistake, or may make a mistake. However, if a mistake is published, the newspaper will correct it as soon as possible.

5. *hardy* (1): robust, strong
    perennial (1): persistent, recurrent
    on-deck circle (6): in baseball, the area where the next batter warms up (in other words, the article is next to be published)
    expletives (9): obscene or profane words or phrases
    assertions (12): declarations, affirmations
    adhering (14): sticking
    readability (16): the quality of being easily read
    venue (23): place, locale

Questions About the Writer's Craft (p. 294)

1. The audience for Shipley's essay is the readers of the New York *Times*. Since the *Times* has a national circulation and is read by those in government circles, this is a broad group of people, many of them important. The topic is of interest to New York *Times* readers mostly because they gain a better understanding of the vetting that op-ed pieces undergo but also because some of them may themselves submit articles for the op-ed page and will then undergo this editing process. Shipley's process analysis is informational; he is educating his readers about the process but is not instructing them on how to do it themselves.

2. The first set of tasks involves checking for grammar, typos, style, length, and accuracy, the "clear-cut things" introduced in paragraph 7. When a fact is called into question, the author's assertion about it is checked (12). The second set of tasks

107

involves improving the readability of the essay, introduced in paragraph 16. This includes adding clarifications, smoothing transitions, cutting digressions, moving copy, and simplifying the language. The third set of tasks involves communicating editorial changes to the writer and negotiating any differences between the editor and the writer in order to finalize the piece. Shipley divides the overall editing process into these main components because each is a fundamentally different type of task. The first is largely cut-and-dried, the second involves more editorial judgment, and the third focuses on the communication between the editor and the writer.

3. According to Shipley, if a fact-checker finds a discrepancy between a fact and one of the writer's assertions, the writer will be challenged to prove the accuracy of the assertion. If he cannot, then he has to find some other evidence to support his argument, and the editor will offer guidance. In the example, the writer has made an assertion—that the police in his town have no reason to change their tactics—that is not borne out by the fact that the town crime rate is rising. Since the facts show that the police *do* have reason to change their tactics, the writer must come up with another suggestion for dealing with the crime problem. The example is effective because it adds to the reader's understanding of the depth of the editing an op-ed piece undergoes. Fact-checking is not merely a matter of gauging the accuracy of individual facts; it also involves checking the reasoning in an article.

4. Shipley's small joke in the concluding paragraph is that he, too, is subject to the editorial process when he writes an essay for the op-ed page, even though normally he is the one doing the editing. He is acknowledging the writer's, rather than the editor's, point of view on the editorial process by indicating he wouldn't accept all the suggested editorial changes on this article. This brings the article to a satisfying end because it makes it seem that the writer has the last word, after all, even though in fact the *Times* editors have the last word—they can always refuse to publish an article.

ANSWERS FOR CHAPTER 15
"COMPARISON-CONTRAST" (p. 298)

OPENING COMMENTS

Students learn early that comparison-contrast questions are one of the mainstays of essay exams: "Compare and/or contrast the organization of the Senate and the House of Representatives"; "Discuss the similarities and/or differences between psychotic and neurotic behavior."

We've found that students' familiarity with comparison-contrast doesn't necessarily mean they know how to structure their answers. On the contrary, many students tend to prepare helter-skelter papers that ramble every which way and back. Yet once they are introduced to some basic strategies for organizing a comparison-contrast discussion, their overall ability to write clearly and logically often takes a quantum leap.

When first learning to use comparison-contrast, students may be overly concerned about making their ideas fit into a neat symmetrical pattern; they may try to squeeze their points into an artificial and awkward format. We find it helpful to remind students that comparison-contrast is not an end in itself but a strategy for meeting a broader rhetorical purpose. Our reminder loosens them up a bit and encourages them to be more flexible when organizing their papers. The student essay "The Virtues of Growing Older" (pages 309–10) helps students appreciate that a well-organized comparison-contrast paper does not have to follow a rigid formula.

We selected the readings in this chapter because, in addition to being just plain interesting, all of them illustrate key points about the comparison-contrast format. In "Euromail and Amerimail," Weiner employs both comparison-contrast strategies in his essay about e-mail. To illustrate her point that classic novels and reality-TV dating shows have much in common, Cohen ("Reality TV: Surprising Throwback to the Past?") utilizes the point-by-point method of comparison to build a compelling case. And in "Friending, Ancient or Otherwise," Wright compares social-networking communities to tribal societies.

ACTIVITIES: COMPARISON-CONTRAST

Below we provide possible responses to selected activities at the end of Chapter 15. Of course, other approaches are possible.

Prewriting Activities (p. 313)

1. There are numerous ways to use comparison-contrast in these two essays. Below are some possibilities. In going over this activity in class, we suggest you have students trade responses so that they can see how diverse the responses are.

   Topic: The effects of holding a job in college

   > Comparing/contrasting job-holders' and non-job-holders' grades
   > Comparing/contrasting on-campus and off-campus jobs
   > Comparing/contrasting part-time and full-time jobs
   > Comparing/contrasting job-holders' and non-job-holders' involvement in campus activities

   Topic: How to budget money wisely

   > Comparing/contrasting formal and informal budgets
   > Comparing/contrasting following a budget to buying on impulse
   > Comparing/contrasting those who budget and those who don't
   > Comparing/contrasting reasonable and unreasonable budgets

2. Here are some possible purposes for the topics.

   a. Videotapes and DVDs
   To guide student purchases
   To explain the technologies

   b. Paper or plastic bags at the supermarket
   To contrast the environmental impact of each
   To help students decide which to use

   c. Two courses taught by inexperienced and "pro" instructors
   To argue a novice may convey more enthusiasm for a subject
   To give students information for choosing courses

    d.   Cutting class and not showing up at work
        To illustrate the consequences of irresponsibility
        To show the similarities and differences between college and the "real world"

Revising Activities (p. 314)

5. a. This statement works well as a thesis.

    b. This statement is unworkable as a thesis; it is too vague and broad since "assistance" could refer to academic, financial, or other kinds of aid. A possible revision: "This college provides much more comprehensive job-placement services to students than other colleges in the area."

    c. This statement would be effective as a thesis if revised to state an attitude toward the candidates' use of television, for example, if one made legitimate use of the medium and the other none. A possible revision: "Joe Cooper's overwrought campaign tactics gained extensive media coverage, while Cooper's opponent, Nancy Ashbury, conducted a more subdued campaign that emphasized issues and failed to attract much attention."

    d. This statement would not work as a thesis. First of all, it points out the obvious and sets up the writer for a pedantic recital of known information. Secondly, the statement is far too inclusive; in attempting to cover the topic, the writer would have to use a ream of paper. A possible revision: "Applying their technological know-how, Japanese car manufacturers learned how to make small engines more powerful, while American companies, showing very little foresight, simply added power to their cars by reintroducing larger engines."

6. Have students read each other's version of this paragraph so that they get a stronger sense of what changes needed to be made and the revision strategies possible.

Here are the main problems with the paragraph:

— Since the paragraph discusses a boss and then a manager, the topic sentence should be reversed to read, "A boss discourages staff resourcefulness and views it as a threat, while a manager encourages creativity and treats employees courteously."

— The second sentence ("At the hardware store . . .") begins abruptly; a transition, such as "for example," would be helpful here.

— The boss's helter-skelter system is introduced awkwardly: "What he did was. . . ." Something like this might be more effective: "He organized overstocked items. . . ."

— The phrase "created chaos" is vague, possibly a bit extreme, and also somewhat slangy. Briefly describing the actual problems his system created would be helpful, as long as the paragraph doesn't veer offtrack and focus entirely on the chaos.

— Some language is possibly too judgmental: "helter-skelter" (4), "slapdash" (7), and "eccentric" (9). Students may want to describe the system with enough telling details so the readers can see for themselves the system's inefficiency.

— No reason is given for the boss's anger at the new system—or perhaps there was no reason other than that his ego was deflated. In either case, the source of his objections should be clarified.

— Some ideas are repeated at the end; sentences 8 and 9 ("I had assumed he would welcome my ideas. . .") repeat material conveyed at the beginning of the paragraph.

— The phrase "to scrap" is perhaps a bit slangy in tone.

112

EUROMAIL AND AMERIMAIL

Eric Weiner

Questions for Close Reading (p. 317)

1. Weiner states his thesis in the first sentence: "North America and Europe are two continents divided by a common technology: e-mail."

2. Weiner describes the characteristics of Amerimail in the second paragraph. He indicates that Amerimail is informal, chatty, and colloquial, often with smiley faces and "xoxo's." It contains a lot of information that's unnecessary. He also characterizes it as being paradoxically "rambling and yet direct; deferential, yet arrogant." In contrast, Euromail is stiff, cold, formal, businesslike, and polite (paragraph 3).

3. Weiner describes several sources of frustration when Americans and Europeans communicate by e-mail. First, Americans tend to respond quickly to e-mail if they respond at all; Europeans respond slowly, but reliably. Second, Americans often mix business and personal matters in e-mail, whereas Europeans keep their personal and business e-mail separate. Third, Americans tend to view e-mail like the telephone, so they write whatever comes to mind; Europeans view e-mail as a type of business letter, so they are very focused. Fourth, Americans are more careful about e-mail security; Europeans view it as a confidential medium. Because each group tends to expect the other group to use e-mail in the same way it does, frustration occurs because the correspondent does not live up to expectations.

4. Weiner prefers Euromail because it is more deliberate, formal, and polite. He does so because he's grown tired of reading rambling, incoherent, and lengthy e-mail messages from Americans and would be happy instead with a few well-chosen words.

5. *hapless* (2): unfortunate
   deferential (2): showing respect and esteem
   brusque (3): short, abrupt, blunt
   confrontational (3): oppositional
   overt (3): open to view
   bottom line (12): net profit
   fastidiousness (14): the quality of having high and often capricious

standards; of being hard to please
lax (14): not strict
cogent (15): convincing, relevant
missives (15): letters

Questions About the Writer's Craft (p. 317)

1. The technology-related words in the first paragraph serve to emphasize the array of modern communications media, and the modernity and sophistication of our present means of communication. This dominant impression is then dismantled in the rest of the essay as Weiner turns his focus on the human aspects of e-mail communication that cause cross-cultural difficulties.

2. Weiner uses the point-by-point method of organization as follows:

    Amerimail: informal and chatty
    Euromail: stiff, formal, and cold
    Amerimail: colloquial
    Euromail: not checked as frequently
    Amerimail: fast response
    Euromail: e-mailing is in place of writing business letters
    Amerimail: e-mailing is in place of telephoning
    Amerimail: unreliable
    Euromail: reliable
    Euromail: less time spent on it
    Amerimail: hours spent on it
    Amerimail: fast response
    Euromail: slow, thoughtful response
    Euromail: full of business secrets
    Amerimail: more discreet

    Alternatively, Weiner could have made all his points about Amerimail in the first part of the essay and all his points about Euromail in the second part of the essay. This probably would not have been as effective, because readers would find it hard to keep all of Amerimail's characteristics in mind when reading about Euromail. The point-by-point organization is more effective for this essay.

3. Weiner uses a transitional expression when shifting between Amerimail and Euromail points only once, in paragraph 12, when he says, "Americans, *by*

114

comparison, spend two hours…" Otherwise he simply describes an aspect of Amerimail, then describes an aspect of Euromail. This may be because Weiner wrote the essay to be delivered on the radio. When reading it aloud, he uses pauses and changes of intonation to signal the listener. These cues are lost when the essay is read. In fact, the essay would be smoother and easier to read if it used transitional expressions between the points of comparison and contrast.

4. Weiner uses a recommendation or call for action to conclude the essay. He indicates he would be pleased if Americans adopted the style of Euromail so that his in-box wouldn't be cluttered with lengthy, digressive, and chatty messages. Most students will find this conclusion surprising, since Weiner is an American and one would expect he would be more comfortable with Amerimail rather than Euromail.

REALITY TV: SURPRISING THROWBACK TO THE PAST?

Patricia Cohen

Questions for Close Reading (p. 322)

1. The selection's main idea is expressed in the second paragraph: "But there's something familiar about the fortune hunters, the status seekers, the thwarted loves, the meddling friends, the public displays, the comic manners, and the sharp competitiveness [on reality-TV dating shows]—all find their counterparts in [the novels of] Jane Austen and Edith Wharton." In other words, there are remarkable similarities between current reality-TV dating shows and the plots of Victorian and Edwardian novels. This thesis is reiterated in the essay's concluding paragraph: "In the end, the American public will choose Lisa's potential spouse in what could be seen simply as a more democratic version of those literary heroes and heroines who gave themselves wholly over to society and allowed their extended family to pick an appropriate mate."

2. Cohen indicates that the general perception among critics is quite negative. She says, in paragraph 2, "To many critics, *Cupid* and other matchmaking shows that mix money and real-life marital machinations represent a cynical and tasteless new genre that is yet another sign of America's moral decline." Later, she observes that the gamut of dating shows "have all been scorned for debasing the sanctity of marriage and for their shallow, indecorous exhibitionism" (11). While Cohen may agree that some tactics on these shows are unsavory, she clearly disagrees with the fundamental

115

basis of critics' displeasure. She asserts in her thesis that there's nothing new about reality-TV's mix of "money and real-life marital machinations," which, she argues, finds inspiration in novels of more than a century ago. She says that "there's something familiar about the fortune hunters, the status seekers, the thwarted loves, the meddling friends, the public displays, the comic manners, and the sharp competitiveness—all find their counterparts in Jane Austen and Edith Wharton" (2). Cohen seems to warn overzealous critics to get off their high horse and to be aware of the long tradition of communal courtship before they attack reality shows on such grounds.

3. The following are among the many similarities Cohen draws between reality-TV dating shows and the plots of classic novels:
   - Today's brief studio tryouts parallel the three-minute waltzes of yesteryear (2).
   - Like many of Austen's heroines, Lisa Shannon has entrusted others with finding her an appropriate suitor (3).
   - Both genres share the implicit assumption that a woman who is not married by her late twenties is doomed to be an old maid (3).
   - In both contexts, money plays a large and openly discussed role (4).
   - Friends play the important roles of judge and protector in the TV shows and in the novels (5).
   - These same friends supply "piquant social commentary, deliciously wicked judgments, and intrigue" (6) in both genres.
   - In both situations, friends don't always agree in their evaluations (7).

4. Cohen refers to one difference between the two early in the essay when she mentions in passing that "Lisa Shannon may lack the wit, depth, and cleverness of an Austen heroine" (3). But it is later on, in paragraphs 12 and 13, that Cohen discusses some more significant differences. Whereas courtship rituals of previous times featured more of a communal sense, today's dating scene has an "individualistic, go-it-alone ethic" (12). Individuals seeking a mate today "are pretty much left to their own devices to suss out partners," whereas the Victorians and Edwardians organized a wide array of social events "to help their younger members find mates" (12). Cohen concludes the essay by mentioning the single most significant difference between the past and the present: Today, a woman can obtain a no-fault divorce if it turns out the match isn't a good one (13).

5. *suitor* (1): man who is seeking the affection of a woman
   machinations (2): crafty schemes
   cynical (2): believing that people are motivated chiefly by base or selfish concerns
   thwarted (2): defeated through opposition

counterparts (2): corresponding things

waltzes (2): ballroom dance in triple time with a strong accent on the first beat

ethos (3): fundamental values belonging to a specific person or culture

dowry (4): money or property brought by a bride to her husband at marriage

mien (4): bearing or manner

eponymous (4): having a name based directly on another name

animation (4): filled with liveliness

gold diggers (5): people who seek money from someone of the opposite sex

piquant (6): appealingly provocative

intrigue (6): secret or underhanded scheme

sabotaging (6): acting treacherously to defeat or hinder a cause

confidante (6): one to whom secrets or private matters are disclosed

unanimous (7): sharing the same opinion

prosaic (7): dull

sparring (7): dispute

debasing (11): degrading

indecorous (11): lacking propriety or good taste

exhibitionism (11): act of deliberately behaving so as to attract attention

courtship (12): process of gaining the love or affection of another

suss out (12): sizing up or figuring out

protagonists (13): main character in a literary work

Questions About the Writer's Craft (p. 323)

1. Cohen uses the point-by-point method of organization in comparing reality-TV dating shows and the plots of classic novels. This method helps emphasize the remarkable similarities between the two seemingly different cultural artifacts. By repeatedly juxtaposing the surprisingly similar elements of the two, Cohen offers proof of her thesis: that reality-TV dating shows are part of a classic literary and social tradition and that, by extension, the shows might not be as tasteless and immoral as critics make them out to be.

2. Cohen seems to anticipate a reader who, at least at first glance, disagrees with her premise. She seems to imagine an audience that concurs with "many critics" in believing that reality-TV dating shows "represent a cynical and tasteless new genre that is yet another sign of America's moral decline" (2). The fact that Cohen addresses this critical view of the shows so early in her essay suggests that she believes it's the prevailing perception. In so doing, Cohen uses Rogerian strategy, seeking to acknowledge and disarm her opposition.

3. The majority of quotations that Cohen provides in her essay are from primary sources—the TV show (*Cupid*, in paragraphs 6, 7, 10, and 12) and the classic books (*Pride and Prejudice*, *Emma*, and *The House of Mirth*, in paragraphs 4, 8, 9, and 12) that compose Cohen's comparison. Cohen quotes these sources directly in order to offer specific proof of her thesis—that the two genres she's comparing do, in fact, share similarities. Providing summaries or paraphrasing would have been much less compelling or convincing, as well as somewhat tedious for readers. The other type of quotation she provides is from a secondary source: Richard Kaye, an English professor and expert on Victorian and Edwardian fiction. While Cohen paraphrases much of what Kaye believes, she directly quotes his admission that he is a "guilty watcher" of the shows. This key verbatim admission from an expert lends credibility to Cohen's thesis—though a more extensive quotation would likely have served the thesis even better.

4. In seeking to explain differences between old-fashioned courtship and today's dating, Cohen provides insight into reasons why things have changed. She says that the "formal social arrangements" of the Victorian and Edwardian times—including "balls, dinners, afternoon teas, country walks, and the like"—no longer exist. The consequence of this is that today's singles are "left to their own devices to suss out partners" (12). While the marriage market remains as "brutally competitive" as it once was, the "individualistic, go-it-alone ethic of modern courtship" and the falling away of "elaborate courtship rituals" leave many individuals unsure of where and how to find a mate. And, according to Cohen, today's high divorce rate is the costly result of society's individualistic rather than communally oriented courtship rituals.

FRIENDING, ANCIENT OR OTHERWISE

Alex Wright

Questions for Close Reading (p. 326)

1. The thesis is given in two parts. In paragraph 1, Wright asks, "But is this world [of social networks] as new as it seems?" He gives something of an answer in the last paragraph: "Still, the sheer popularity of social networking seems to suggest that for many, these environments strike a deep, perhaps even primal chord." Taken together, these statements express the main idea: Social-networking communities

118

attempt, as shown by their similarities to more traditional societies, to fulfill some of the most elemental needs that people have.

2. Wright suggests that social networking seems to fulfill an innate desire humans have to talk to one another. He characterizes online communication—"blog posts, comments, homemade videos and, lately, an outpouring of epigrammatic one-liners broadcast using services like Twitter and Facebook status updates"—as an "outpouring of expression that often feels more like 'talking' than writing" (5). While not saying so explicitly, he implies that the growth of social networks points to some success in their ability to meet what one researcher calls "deep-seated, prehistoric patterns of human communication" (5).

3. Wright says that some academics are "exploring the parallels between online social networks and tribal societies" (3) to better understand the "social-networking phenomenon" (7). He quotes one researcher who calls oral communication the "base of all human experience" (4) and another who asserts that oral communication "unites people in groups" (7). Wright concludes that in any human group, oral communication is more than "just talking": in oral communication we see "social dynamics at work" (8).

4. Wright asks whether the characteristics of online relationships will "begin to shape the way" people relate to one another in the real world (17). He quotes one researcher who "worries" that social networking "may be gobbling up what's left of our real oral culture" (18). While not strongly denouncing such an outcome, Wright clearly suggests that the growth of social networking raises a real issue about the nature of social bonding in the future.

5. *resurgence* (3): rebirth
   epigrammatic (5): having the quality of a short, usually witty, saying
   participatory (6): providing the chance for everyone to take part
   interactive (6): mutually responding to or affecting one another
   cadences (7): rhythmic patterns of sound, as in music or speech
   prescient (7): having foresight or foreknowledge
   ethnographic (9): pertaining to the branch of anthropology that studies individual cultures
   antecedent (13): something that precedes another thing
   proximity (14): nearness
   simulates (15): imitates
   formalized (16): characterized by tradition, convention, or ceremoniousness

Questions About the Writer's Craft (p. 327)

1. Wright uses the point-by-point method to compare interpersonal communication in tribal societies and social-networking communities.

    First, he explores the ways, according to researchers, that the communities are similar: "messaging and 'friending'" mimic the oral communication in tribal societies (4); "how people know you" establishes a person's identity for both social networks and traditional groups (10); and giving gifts, whether "ritual objects" or Facebook's "symbolic sock monkeys," helps "cement ... social ties" (11).

    Then Wright points out the ways in which the groups differ: in tribal groups forging social bonds is a "matter of survival," while in "virtual" communities doing so is less important (13); in traditional communities "ongoing face-to-face" communications result in real friendships (14), while on the Internet "distance" creates "weak ties" with "the appearance of a connection" (15); and in tribal cultures members participate in "highly formalized rituals," while social-network members typically treat one another with a "casualness and familiarity" that they would not use in real-world situations (16).

2. Wright's primary evidence is expert opinion, which he cites in nine of nineteen paragraphs. In all, he quotes four researchers, explaining their work and giving their credentials: Lance Strate, "a communications professor at Fordham University and devoted MySpace user" (4); Irwin Chen, "a design instructor at Parsons who is developing a new course to explore the emergence of oral culture online" (6); the Rev. Walter J. Ong, "a professor at St. Louis University and student of Marshall McLuhan" (7); and Michael Wesch, "who teaches cultural anthropology at Kansas State University, [and] spent two years living with a tribe in Papua New Guinea, studying how people forge social relationships in a purely oral culture" (9). The use of expert opinion is very effective. Wright uses quotations from experts to support nearly every point he makes.

3. How to define *friend* is an important issue in the article. In paragraph 14, Wright says, "Then there's the question of who really counts as a 'friend.' " Before that, he asks, Can we "make 'friends' with people we barely know" (1)? Wright often puts the word *friend* in quotation marks, as if he is using it ironically or ambivalently. One researcher makes the point that in both tribal societies and online communities "You define yourself in terms of who your friends are" (10). But Wright seems to suggest that if people have always needed "direct, ongoing face-to-face contact" (14) to become friends, can we really call our "hyperlinked 'friends'" (18) true friends: Can we "stretch the definition of a friend to encompass people we may never actually meet" (18)?

In paragraph 17, Wright signals the use of cause-effect with the term "paradoxical consequence." One researcher questions—and Wright also wonders—whether the growth of social networking will cause "the strength of our real-world friendships [to] grow diluted" (18). The author doesn't answer this question, but his use of cause and effect here invests the topic with urgency and echoes the questioning approach he uses to establish his thesis.

4. The first part of the conclusion—"Still, the sheer popularity of social networking seems to suggest that for many, these environments strike a deep, perhaps even primal chord"—answers the question posed in paragraph 3 and can thus be seen as part of the thesis statement. Then, to conclude the essay, Wright employs the strategy of using a quotation from an expert, one whom he has already quoted extensively to support his main points. The strong quotation—"We all want to be told: You exist"—powerfully reminds the reader of the important issues at stake.

ANSWERS FOR CHAPTER 16
"CAUSE-EFFECT" (p. 331)

OPENING COMMENTS

Along with comparison-contrast, cause-effect writing (often called "causal analysis") is frequently required of college students—especially in exam situations. ("Analyze the causes of the country's spiraling divorce rate"; "Discuss the impact of the revised tax laws on middle-income families.") Since students can't deny that an ability to write sound causal analyses will serve them well, they're generally eager to tackle this pattern of development.

Not surprisingly, though, many students run into problems with their analyses. Although they enjoy the intellectual challenge of tracing causes and effects, they sometimes stop at the obvious—overly concerned as they are about getting closure on an issue.

We've found a classroom activity that helps counteract this urge to oversimplify. Here's what we do. We put on the board a broad, noncontroversial statement. (For example, "In the United States, many people work hard to keep physically fit.") Then we ask students to take five minutes (we time them and announce when the time is up) to brainstorm the reasons *why* (causes) people are so involved in physical fitness. Then we ask students to spend another five minutes brainstorming the *consequences* (effects) of this concern with physical fitness. Next we put students in pairs and then in groups of four; each time, they exchange first their causes and then their effects. As you'd expect, this activity generates a good deal of energy. We hear a number of comments, such as, "That's interesting. I never thought of that." Such a reaction is precisely what we hope for. The activity sensitizes students to the complexity of cause-effect relationships and encourages them to dig deeply and not settle for the obvious.

For this chapter, we chose professional selections that dramatize the power of causal analysis to make the reader think. In his essay "Why We Crave Horror Movies," King, a master of horror himself, considers both the obvious and the underlying reasons for the horror film's popularity. Kleiner examines the causes and effects of procrastination ("When Mañana Is Too Soon"), and Staples ("Black Men and Public Space") describes the corrosive effects of racism on his life.

ACTIVITIES: CAUSE-EFFECT

Below we provide possible responses to selected activities at the end of Chapter 16. Of course, other approaches are possible.

Prewriting Activities (p. 347)

1. There are many ways to use cause-effect in these two essays; the lists below suggest only a few of the possibilities. We suggest that you have students share their ideas on ways to use cause-effect in these essays. Seeing others' ideas makes the point dramatically that writing involves invention and individuality.

    Topic: The need for a high-school course in personal finance

    > Causes of many young people's casual attitude to money
    > Causes of parents' reluctance to teach about finance
    > Effects of a young person bouncing checks
    > Effects of overspending

    Topic: How to show appreciation

    > Causes of people's callous disregard for each other
    > Causes of an appreciative approach to good manners
    > Effects of appreciation in everyday life
    > Effects of not showing appreciation

2. Here are some possible causes and/or effects for the various topics. Others are possible. In the second part of the activity, outlining will depend upon the points generated.

    a. Pressure on students to do well

    Causes:
    > High career ambitions
    > Parental demands
    > Inner pressure; self-esteem

    Effects:
    > Restricted social, campus, and physical activities
    > Emotional instability, anger
    > Less-effective academic performance

b. Being physically fit

Causes:

Media attention to health concerns

Trend to engage in sports

Desire to look attractive

Effects:

Better health

Growing enrollments in health clubs

Preoccupation with fitness

c. Spiraling costs of college education

Causes:

Growing costs of faculty and staff

Modernization going on: computers, for example

Inflation

Cutbacks in state and federal funds

Effects:

Students burdened with more loans

Concern about paying back loans influences career choices

More students work during college

Some students drop out

Revising Activities (p. 348)

4. a. The growing Latin American immigrant population and the crime rate may be correlated—that is, there may be some connection between the two. That both figures are increasing, however, does not mean that the rise in immigration has *caused* the rise in crime. To say so is *post hoc* thinking.

   b. This statement shows *post hoc* thinking because it assumes that one of two parallel events is causing the other—that is, that more women working is causing the divorce rate to rise. However, there are other possible reasons for the increase in the divorce rate: a change in American values regarding the family, for instance, or the "sexual revolution." Moreover, one could cite the same two facts—more women working and the divorce rate rising—and argue the opposite, that the divorce rate is causing more women to work outside the home. In any case, disregarding these other possible points of view and arguing that a clear-cut relationship necessarily exists is an example of *post hoc* thinking.

124

c. These two parallel situations do not have a proven causal relationship. To say that one has caused the other is *post hoc* reasoning, unless other proof exists. Such proof might consist of information about what chemicals exist in the landfill; whether they are cancer causing; whether the chemicals have leached into the soil, water, or air of the town; and whether other causes for the cancer might exist.

5. It's a good idea to provide time in class for students to read over each other's revisions of this paragraph. Seeing how others handled the activity can give students a stronger sense of their revision options.

Here are the main problems with the paragraph:

— Overall, the paragraph asserts that the bank machines have caused certain behaviors and attempts to support such a claim with broad generalizations stated in absolute terms. For example, the fourth sentence asserts that automatic tellers have negatively influenced the "average individual." Similarly, the next three sentences state—almost categorically—that people, once they have cash readily in hand, invariably spend their lunch hours shopping. Equivalent absolutes can be found throughout. The paragraph could be rescued if the writer toned down the absolute tone and provided qualifications that suggest that "for some people" or "for many people" these machines present problems.

— The writer assumes causation explains the circumstances (use of ATM cards and people shopping during lunch hour) when these may simply be correlated—that is, they may happen at the same time because they are two results of some other earlier event. Or the simultaneous appearance of increased spending and ATM-card use may be a coincidence, meaning that the writer has committed the *post hoc* fallacy.

— Another problem with the paragraph is its lack of supporting examples. Although it isn't necessary for the writer to provide hard evidence in the form of research, he or she should have supported the paragraph with specific references to friends, family, et al for whom automatic tellers have created problems.

— The point that children don't appreciate the value of money is an unfounded generalization; it also digresses from the paragraph's point and so should be eliminated.

— The last sentence categorically asserts ("There's no doubt. . .") that banking-machine fraud is a cause of the "immoral climate in the country." This is an unsupported causal statement and would need evidence to be considered valid. It should be deleted.

WHY WE CRAVE HORROR MOVIES

Stephen King

Questions for Close Reading (p. 351)

1. King states the *topic* of his essay clearly in the title, which proposes to explore not only why we watch or enjoy horror movies but why we *crave* them. He does not, however, state his *thesis* explicitly but rather develops over the course of the essay his main idea: that the horror movie satisfies a type of "insanity in us." He begins with the provocative opinion, "I think we're all mentally ill; those of us outside the asylum only hide it a little better" (paragraph 1). For King, sanity is only "a matter of degree," and we are all on the same continuum as "Jack the Ripper or the Cleveland Torso Murderer" (8). While King is sure that "the potential lyncher is in all of us" (9), he also knows that society works very hard to hide or repress this fact. As a result, "every now and then, [the lyncher] has to be let loose" (9). It is what King calls the "dirty job" of horror movies to satisfy "all that is worst in us" (12). Watching these movies is like "throwing a basket of raw meat to the hungry alligators swimming around in that subterranean river beneath" (12). King concludes that horror movies keep the dangerous psychological gators "down there" and a more ostensibly sane "me up here" (13).

2. In paragraph 8, King wants to collapse the separation between the sane and the insane. Watching a horror movie, we are all invited to "lapse into simplicity, irrationality, and even outright madness" (7) as we enjoy the spectacle of "seeing others menaced—sometimes killed" (6). Our eager participation in this "modern version of the public lynching" (6) proves that "we are all insane" and that, by extension, "sanity becomes a matter of degree" (8). The infamous killers are now invoked to demonstrate this point. Using the second person, King directly addresses the reader, placing him or her on a continuum with famous killers. King writes, "if your insanity leads you to carve up women like Jack the Ripper or the Cleveland Torso Murderer, we clap you away in the funny farm . . . if, on the other hand your insanity leads you only to talk to yourself"—or to crave horror films—"then you are

126

left alone" (8). The extreme examples of the serial murderers are necessary to illustrate King's main thesis: the presence of a shared "insanity of man," which the horror movie satisfies (11). Linking the psychopath and supposedly normal everyday people (like us) is King's project, and the references to the murderers in paragraph 8 establish this uncomfortable bond.

3. What King calls the "conservative" nature of horror movies should not be understood in terms of politics. Instead, King uses the term more strictly to mean "cautious," "traditional," and "staid." While horror films may challenge us to face the darkness, they provide no new understanding of it. King argues that horror movies "re-establish our feelings of essential normality" (4). By watching monsters on the screen, we reassure ourselves that we are not monsters ourselves. As King writes, horror movies remind us that "no matter how far we may be removed from the beauty of a Robert Redford or a Diana Ross, we are still light-years from true ugliness," such as that of the grotesque creatures featured in many films (4). Furthermore, King argues that horror movies encourage us to "put away our more civilized and adult penchant for analysis" and to see the world in "pure blacks and whites" (7). In reinforcing basic definitions like "us" and "them," horror movies touch on the "reactionary," restoring us to primal, absolute attitudes and emotions.

    Yet some of these same impulses inspired by horror movies render the films "anarchistic, and revolutionary" (11)—quite the opposite of conservative. Reveling in the dark fun of horror movies, we "exercise" our inherent universal "anti-civilization emotions" (11)—the ones that society attempts to quash out of us, as in the example of the child being punished for deliberately hurting "the little rotten puke of a sister" (10). The "dirty job" of horror movies is highly subversive in nature: "It is morbidity unchained, our most basic instincts let free, our nastiest fantasies realized" (12). As we watch these films, "we may allow our emotions a free rein . . . or no rein at all" (7). So while horror films may restore our conservative sense of humanity (as opposed to the extreme monstrousness on the screen), they also incite an anarchy of the psyche, where our delight in the grotesque is free from regulation. In spite of the "civilized forebrain," horror movies feed "the hungry alligators swimming around in that subterranean river beneath" (12).

4. Alligators symbolize the latent uncivilized tendencies that King argues we all possess but are compelled, by society, to repress. Throughout his essay, King develops his theory that sanity is only "a matter of degree" and that we are all on the same continuum as "Jack the Ripper or the Cleveland Torso Murderer" (8). Society, however, militates against "the potential lyncher . . . in all of us" (9). It encourages actions based on feelings like "love, friendship, loyalty, kindness," while actively discouraging their opposites (10). To King's mind, however, sanctioned emotions are

127

only half of the equation; the rest of our emotions—the aberrant ones—won't disappear, and they too "demand periodic exercise" (11). So, while love may be the sort of emotion endorsed by society, this and other benevolent sentiments cannot be sustained unless we periodically satisfy the other, darker elements in our psyche—the "gators." King argues that one safe way to "feed" these gators is to indulge in horror movies, which function as a safety valve for our potentially destructive emotions.

5. *hysterical* (1): characterized by nervous, emotional outbursts
    reactionary (4): extremely conservative; opposed to progress
    voyeur (6): one who is highly stimulated by watching others
    lynching (6): illegal mob action against a person; a murder carried out by a mob
    penchant (7): a strong preference, inclination, or liking
    immortalized (9): made eternal
    anarchistic (11): lawless, wild
    morbidity (12): an interest in gloom, disease, and death

Questions About the Writer's Craft (p. 351)

1. King may be seen, at different points in the essay, as encompassing each of the three purposes. In explaining why we crave horror movies, King proposes a theory of the human psyche. Unlike a scientific researcher, he offers no statistical, biological, or clinical data. He does not aim to inform us about new psychological discoveries. Instead, he acts like a philosopher and *speculates* about the nature of human emotions and, more specifically, about why we crave horror movies. He develops a theory about the existence of a shared "insanity of man," which the horror movie satisfies (11). But he then attempts throughout the rest of the essay to *convince* us of this claim's validity, providing an abundance of vivid examples and analogies. His purpose may also be interpreted as *informative*; King wants to show us the dark, repressed part of ourselves as well as a benign means of keeping it at bay: watching horror movies.

    King's theory also functions as a defense of his own craft—of not only why we crave horror movies but why King writes them. In convincing us of our psychological need for horror movies, he simultaneously (and implicitly) seeks to convince us of our practical need for horror writers—like King himself.

2. The task of King's essay is to spell out the dark psychological tendencies satisfied by horror movies. In order to explain the "simple and obvious" (3) reasons for the horror film's attraction, King begins by comparing it to a roller coaster. Like roller coasters, horror movies pose a challenge. As King argues, in both cases "we are daring the nightmare" (2), and we do so "to show that we can, that we are not afraid" (3). In

both, we enjoy the sheer thrill of the ride—the possibility that a movie, like a coaster ride, might "surprise a scream out of us" (3) or might just be "fun" (5). But, according to King, horror films fundamentally differ from roller coasters in the source of all that fun. Our enjoyment of horror movies, he demonstrates, originates in a far darker and more complex part of the psyche. In the horror movie, the fun comes not from twists and turns but from "seeing others menaced—sometimes killed" (6). The horror movie returns us to childlike thinking, shutting down adult analysis and recasting the world in "pure blacks and whites" (7). In this way, horror movies invite us "to lapse into simplicity, irrationality, and outright madness" (7). Roller coasters, by implication, do not serve nearly as complicated a function.

King then turns to a second comparison-contrast to explain our response to horror movies. He says that "the horror film has become the modern form of the public lynching" (6). In both cases, spectators derive "a very peculiar sort of fun . . . from seeing others menaced—sometimes killed" (6). This malignant pleasure in morbidity always lurks beneath our socially adjusted surfaces, King argues, but society systematically represses these "anti-civilization emotions" (11). The implied difference between the two is that public lynchings are no longer sanctioned by society, while horror movies still are, even though they exercise the same emotions. As King concludes, horror movies keep the dark side "from getting out, man" (13).

King develops a final comparison-contrast to explain the phenomenon of horror movies: the same "anti-civilization emotions" that fuel our enjoyment of the films also incite us to delight in "sick jokes" (11). Sick jokes "may surprise a laugh or a grin out of us even as we recoil" (11)—a response much like the one King attributes to horror-movie watching. He goes a step further in stating that "[t]he mythic horror movie, like the sick joke, has a dirty job to do. It deliberately appeals to all that is worst in us" (12). Our morbid enjoyment of the two serves as evidence of King's larger observation that "we're all mentally ill" (1) and "share in an insanity of man" (11). Another similarity between them is that they both are particularly attractive to young people. Early in the essay, he identifies horror movies as "the special province of the young" (3). Later in the essay, King cites the example of the dead-baby joke that he heard "originally from a ten-year-old" (11). Ultimately, both horror movies and sick jokes attest to the "potential lyncher" (9) that we all harbor within.

3. In explaining our attraction to horror movies, King builds a theory about the shape of our emotional life, a theory that fundamentally includes children. He begins by observing that "horror movies, like roller coasters, have always been the special province of the young" (3). Ostensibly, this youthful appeal owes to the raw thrills provided by both, but King goes on to suggest several less-innocuous reasons for young people's attraction to horror films. In discussing society's repression of malignant human emotions, he cites the example of our youthful reactions to a little

sister (10). King demonstrates how "society showers us with positive reinforcement" (often in the form of sweets) when we exercise valued emotions like love or kindness—"emotions," King explains, "that tend to maintain the status quo" (9). However, when we deliberately hurt "the rotten little puke of a sister," "sanctions follow" (10). King explains the problem of such sanctions in paragraph 11, reminding us that even after a series of punishments "anti-civilization emotions don't go away." We still harbor destructive desires, a fact evidenced in King's example of the "sick joke" told by a 10-year-old. The child's implied enjoyment of the gory "dead baby" joke points to the shared "insanity of man"—King's main point. "We're all mentally ill" (1), he believes, and the perverse impulses that society tries to repress in its young nevertheless remain with us forever. In King's view, children are not innocents; instead, they are an amoral nature run amok. The use of children as examples simply underscores King's belief that "the potential lyncher is in almost all of us" (9).

4. Each of these paragraphs consists solely of one brief sentence or, in the case of paragraph 14, one sentence fragment. In each case, King's compressed writing style adds emphasis and directs our attention to a single idea. In paragraph 2, King places us in the darkened theater, "daring the nightmare," in order to establish the horror movie's conscious and unconscious challenge to viewers. Not only does the film dare us to sit through it, as King will explain in paragraph 3, but the horror movie also dares our darker side to come out and express itself (9). The second brief paragraph—"And we go to have fun" (5)—forces us to think about the unconscious challenge to seek the kind of fun that excites "the potential lyncher . . . in almost all of us" (9). This short paragraph introduces King's thesis about the inherent pleasure involved in "seeing others menaced—sometimes killed" (6). King hopes to deliver the same kind of punch in his sentence-fragment conclusion. In the preceding paragraph, he acknowledges that you, the reader, are taught to believe that civilized emotions are "all you need" (13). But, as his striking conclusion asserts, this is true only "[a]s long as you keep the gators fed" (14). This pithy conclusion, with its vivid imagery, memorably captures King's thesis and promises to resonate in the minds of readers.

WHEN MAÑANA IS TOO SOON

Kurt Kleiner

Questions for Close Reading (p. 356)

1. Kleiner states his thesis in paragraphs 6 and 7, where he indicates that he will be reporting on a review of the literature on procrastination conducted by psychologist Piers Steel. Because "When Mañana Is Too Soon" is a news article reporting on the work of others, rather than an essay about procrastination, the thesis statement is purely informative; it doesn't make a claim, as most of the thesis statements in the other essays in the text do.

2. Steel found that people who procrastinate tend to lack confidence in their ability to do a task, are more impulsive than non-procrastinators, and are less conscientious as well (12). Temporal-motivation theory helps explain the various factors that combine to cause procrastination. Kleiner explains the theory by using an equation (29) and words: "If you expect to fail at a difficult task and you're easily distracted and it doesn't have to be done for quite awhile, you're going to procrastinate" (32).

3. Over the years, psychologists have proposed various ·causes for procrastination: anxiety (9); perfectionism (11); and self sabotage, hostility, depression (26).

4. Kleiner defines procrastination as putting off a task that needs to be done, that will cause problems if it is not done, and that we intend to do (15, 16). Procrastination differs from prioritizing in that it involves an element of irrational behavior—even though we know a task is important and must be done, we put it off.

5. *chronic* (4): constant, habitual, recurring
   mammoth (7): enormous
   impulsive (12): spontaneous
   profoundly (16): deeply, completely
   prolific (17): very inventive and productive
   lexicographer (17): author or editor of a dictionary
   forbear (17): to hold back from, to abstain
   trivialize (24): to make of little worth
   volitional (25): having the power of choosing
   unsettling (33): upsetting

Questions About the Writer's Craft (p. 356)

1. Kleiner lists procrastination's general effects of harm to "work, finances, or personal relationships" (2) and three specific effects of "self-destructive behavior" (3)—money lost by doing taxes at the last minute, possible blindness from glaucoma because of delaying medication, possible health problems for heart patients who delay making lifestyle changes (21–23). But the major focus of the essay is on the possible causes of the procrastination, about which experts disagree. Traditional ideas about causes include self-sabotage, hostility, and rebellion (26) as well as "anxiety, perfectionism and depression" (36). However, a newer idea that Kleiner discusses comes from "behavioural economics" and involves motivation and other factors (27–33).

2. The purpose of Kleiner's article is to inform readers of the newspaper about important new research in the psychology of procrastination by Piers Steel. To achieve his purpose, Kleiner gives Steel's credentials (6) and names the academic journal in which Steel's work appears (7). He then spends another 14 of the 38 paragraphs explaining Steel's ideas. He also cites two psychologists who disagree with Steel (24, 25, 36, 37). So research forms the backbone of Kleiner's essay. Kleiner does a good job of explaining Steel's research. However, there might have been a greater benefit for average readers if Kleiner had more thoroughly explained the idea of the equation and simply left the actual equation out of the article.

3. Other patterns of development include exemplification and definition. In paragraphs 21–23, Kleiner gives three specific examples of the harm procrastination can cause—the cost of putting off doing one's taxes, the potential harm of not taking glaucoma medication, and the health risks of not changing one's lifestyle after a heart attack. In paragraph 31, he gives an example of how the TMT equation might be used to determine whether someone will procrastinate on a particular task. Kleiner defines procrastination in paragraphs 15 and 16 in part by contrasting it with prioritizing tasks.

4. The Samuel Johnson quotations in paragraphs 17 and 18 give the topic of procrastination depth and universality by demonstrating that people have been grappling with it, and trying to understand its causes, for centuries. On the other hand, the quotations slow the reader because they contain dated syntax and vocabulary at odds with the remainder of the news article, with its workmanlike writing style. Deleting these two paragraphs would not detract from the reader's understanding of procrastination, as Kleiner has already shown that it is a universal behavior by citing Cicero and Thucydides in paragraph 2.

132

BLACK MEN AND PUBLIC SPACE

Brent Staples

Questions for Close Reading (p. 359)

1. The closest thing to a direct statement of the thesis occurs in the second paragraph, in the second sentence: "I first began to know the unwieldy inheritance I'd come into— the ability to alter public space in ugly ways."

2. Staples first discovered that other people considered him a threat during his first year away from his hometown, when he was a graduate student in Chicago. There he found that "nighttime pedestrians—particularly women" would run away (2) or cross to the other side of the street (3); people in cars would lock their doors as he crossed the street in front of them (3); doormen, policemen, cabdrivers, and other such workers were unpleasant to him (3). He says he felt "surprised, embarrassed, and dismayed all at once" and "like an accomplice in tyranny" (2). Over time, he gained an awareness that he himself is in danger when he is perceived as dangerous (2). Later in the essay he remarks that there is a "kind of alienation that comes of being ever the suspect" (5).

3. In general, Staples says he has become aware of situations that can be hazardous to him: turning "a corner into a dicey situation"; or crowding "some frightened, armed person in a foyer somewhere"; or making "an errant move after being pulled over by a policeman" (2). Specifically, Staples recounts the most frightening incident, when he was mistaken for a burglar; rushing into a magazine office to deliver an article on deadline, he was pursued through the halls by "an *ad hoc* posse" of employees. In another case, he stopped in a jewelry store to kill time and was confronted by a silent store owner with a huge Doberman pinscher. He handled these nonconfrontationally; in the first case, he dashed to the office of the editor who knew him and could vouch for his honesty. In the second, he simply nodded good night and left the store. He is clearly a nonviolent person.

4. At night and when he is dressed casually, Staples takes care to move slowly and keep a distance from people who look nervous. He avoids giving the appearance of following people when entering buildings. And if he is pulled over by police, he acts extremely friendly and nonthreatening. His final tactic when taking late-night walks

133

is to whistle classical music, communicating that he is educated and has a love of beauty and thus is not a mugger (11–12). These precautions telegraph his real identity: a law-abiding, non-predatory, nonviolent, educated, and cultured person.

5. *uninflammatory* (1): not arousing strong emotion
   dicey (2): risky or uncertain (*informal*)
   bandolier (5): belt with loops for carrying bullets worn over shoulder and across chest
   lethality (6): ability to cause death
   bravado (7): swaggering show of courage; false bravery
   berth (11): (as in "give a wide berth to") avoid
   constitutionals (12): a walk taken for health reasons

Questions About the Writer's Craft (p. 360)

1. The essay concludes with discussions of effects; in paragraph 11, Staples focuses on the effects on him of the perception that he is a mugger. In the last paragraph, he describes the effects on other nighttime pedestrians of his whistling classical melodies. By discussing these effects, Staples shows the inconvenience and foresight necessary for him, and other black men, to go about their daily lives. By mentioning his "excellent tension-reducing measure"—whistling Vivaldi and "the more popular classical composers"—Staples returns to the issue that he began with in the first paragraph and also shows that he has handled a potentially humiliating problem with grace and style.

2. The phrase "my first victim was a woman" is certainly an attention getter, and it may suggest to the reader that the essay narrates a criminal's confession. That Staples goes on to relate a story of misperception shows how quick people are to assume the worst, both on the street and in reading the essay.

3. Staples's audience would seem to be primarily white. Most blacks would know firsthand the problem he writes of; it is the whites who, in encountering him anonymously on the street, need to be told that he, like most black men, is harmless. He signals that his audience is white when he reveals, "Black men trade tales like this all the time" (10). In addition, the essay relies on many references to European tradition: "bandolier" (5), "bravado" (7), "posse" (8), Beethoven, Vivaldi, "cowbells," and "bear country" (12). There are no similar references to black culture.

4. Staples's tone is sad and conciliatory but also tinged with irony. He uses many terms that indicate his unhappiness with his perpetual role as "would-be mugger":

"surprised, embarrassed, and dismayed" (2); "feel like an accomplice in tyranny" (2); "a vast, unnerving gulf" (2); "alienation" (5). He is conciliatory in that he has smothered his rage (11); he attempts to see the other side (5) and the wider perspective (2). That a self-confessed "softy" like him (2) should be taken for a criminal prompts several ironic notes; certainly, his last image, in which he likens himself to an innocent hiker wearing a cowbell to protect himself from "the bears," is strongly ironic.

ACTIVITIES FOR CHAPTER 17
"DEFINITION" (p. 363)

OPENING COMMENTS

In high school and certainly in college, students are frequently asked to answer questions that call for definitions: "Define 'mitosis'"; "Explain what 'divestiture' means." Even so, we hold off discussing definition as a method of development until the last quarter of the course.

Our rationale for delaying definition is based on the need for other patterns of development in fleshing out an extended definition. At the very least, students need to know how to incorporate well-chosen *examples* so that their definitions can be grounded in specifics. Similarly, the *comparison-contrast* format can show students how to go about organizing a definition by negation. And *process analysis*, explaining how something works, can be essential when developing a definition. Once students feel comfortable with these and other strategies, they can approach definition essays with confidence, knowing that they have a repertoire of techniques to draw on.

For this chapter, we selected readings that illustrate a variety of approaches for writing definition essays. Touching on a wide range of topics, the pieces show how definition can explain difficult-to-understand scientific concepts, expand the meaning we attach to everyday words, and help us view our society in a new light. Hulbert ("Beyond the Pleasure Principle") talks about how the attitudes and values of "Gen Nexters" *seem* contradictory but actually make sense. Gleick ("Life As Type A"), in a careful analysis of behavioral research, asserts that the traits typically associated with Type A behavior are actually characteristics we all exhibit. Finally, McCloud ("Setting the Record Straight") uses the medium of a comic book to define what comics actually are.

ACTIVITIES: DEFINITION

Below we provide possible responses to selected activities at the end of Chapter 17. In many cases, other responses are possible.

Prewriting Activities (p. 376)

1. There are many ways to use definition in these two essays. Below we've listed some of the possibilities. In classroom use of this activity, we suggest you have students

share their responses. They will be surprised and often delighted to discover that their neighbors have different answers.

Topic: How to register a complaint

> Define "effective" complaining
> Define a "no-win situation"
> Define "conflict resolution"
> Define "diplomacy"

Topic: Contrasting two stand-up comics

> Define "black humor"
> Define "improvisational humor"
> Define "political humor"
> Define "put-down humor"

2. For this activity, as for 3, students will, of course, each have individual responses. When introducing the activity and discussing students' material, make students aware that their goal is to frame a definition that goes beyond "dictionary meanings" or the commonly understood sense of the term. An essay-worthy personal definition is one that discovers or affirms some less-understood dimension of a word.

Revising Activities (p. 376)

4. Here's our appraisal of the effectiveness of the definitions:

a. This definition is circular because it repeats the words of the term itself. In addition, the "is when" format is awkward, if not ungrammatical. Here's one way to revise the definition: "Passive aggression is a personality disorder in which a person chronically performs poorly as a way of unconsciously showing resentment of the demands of an employer, teacher, or other person."

b. This definition is also ineffective because of its circularity. One way to rewrite it might be this: "A terrorist uses violence against innocent people to intimidate those in power."

c. This definition is effective and clear.

d. This is a circular definition that tells us nothing about the term being defined. A better version would be this: "Pop music typically contains simple lyrics, a strong beat, and appealing harmonies."

e. This definition needs rephrasing to eliminate the awkward "is when"; otherwise, it is a workable definition. "Standing by another person during difficult times is the essence of loyalty."

5. It is a good idea to have your students read each other's revisions of this material. Doing so gives them helpful exposure to alternative ways of rewriting a problem paragraph.

Here are our recommendations for rewriting the paragraph:

— The opening sentence is weak; relying on the dictionary only tells us (boringly) what we already know. The sentence should be rewritten to catch the reader's interest.

— Since the second sentence states the obvious, it should be deleted.

— The listing of times people feel tense (sentences 3, 4, and 5) consists of obvious, general situations. Dramatic examples would be appropriate here.

— Similarly, "Wear and tear on our bodies and on our emotional well-being" is overly general. "Wear and tear" is a cliché as well. Specifying some actual damage that can result from tension would be an effective revision strategy.

— The thesis (how to relieve tension with walking) seems tacked on. A transitional phrase or lead-in is needed to build more naturally to the thesis.

BEYOND THE PLEASURE PRINCIPLE

Ann Hulbert

Questions for Close Reading (p. 379)

1. Hulbert's thesis emerges slowly in this article. Her introduction in paragraphs 1 and 2 serves to narrow the topic of the article, which is stated in the second paragraph: "But if you look closely, what makes Gen Nexters *sui generis*—and perhaps more mysterious than their elders appreciate—are their views on two divisive social topics, abortion and gay marriage." From that point on, Hulbert explores the possible significance of the poll findings on these topics, eventually stating her thesis in paragraph 7: "For when you stop to consider it, at the core of Gen Nexters' seemingly discordant views on these hot-button issues could be an insistence on giving priority to children's interests."

2. The article is based on a report entitled "A Portrait of Generation Next," a survey conducted by the Pew Research Center and MacNeil/Lehrer Productions. In particular, Hulbert focuses on the statistics regarding Gen Nexters' attitudes toward abortion and gay marriage. She points out that on abortion these young people are more conservative than·the general public, but on gay marriage they are more liberal than the general public.

3. In paragraph 5, Hulbert explains these two social-science terms. A "life-cycle effect" is one associated with age; for example, in general, young people tend to be more adventurous than older people. A "cohort effect" is one that is permanently associated with a particular demographic group. For example, the generation that came of age during the Great Depression tended to be thrifty and careful throughout their lives. In this article, Hulbert's thesis is that Gen Nexters' attitudes on abortion and gay marriage will turn out to be part of their cohort's permanent values—a cohort effect rather than a lifestyle effect.

4. According to Hulbert, the baby boomers have failed to "actually think beyond their own welfare to worry about—of all things—the next generation" (7).

5. *tandem* (1): partnership or conjunction
   quintessence (2): the essence of a thing in its purest form
   sui generis (2): of its own kind (Latin); unique
   promiscuous (2): indiscriminate, casual

agnosticism (3): the view that ultimate reality (God) is unknown and unknowable
heterogeneous (5): mixed; dissimilar or diverse
congeal (5): to become rigid and fixed
bulwark (5): a strong support or protection
ethos (6): the distinguishing character or moral nature of a person or group
intransigence (6): the state of being uncompromising
impeded (6): interfered with or slowed the progress of
discordant (7): quarrelsome, disagreeing

Questions About the Writer's Craft (p. 380)

1. Hulbert's purpose in defining Gen Nexters is mainly speculative. From statistics on attitudes toward abortion and gay marriage, Hulbert infers larger qualities and underlying values in Gen Nexters. The language she uses indicates the hypothetical nature of the discussion: "It could simply be …," "But what if …," "Gen Nexters hold what seem …," (paragraph 4); "All this could amount to no more than …," "perhaps," "suggested," "hypothesis" (5); "And to risk what might be truly wishful thinking, maybe there are …," "however you end up sorting the data" (7). In addition, she uses verbs such as *could, would,* and *might* throughout to show that her ideas are provisional.

2. Hulbert uses the definition-by-negation strategy in paragraph 2, where the mixed attitudes of Gen Nexters on abortion and gay marriage are contrasted with those of the typical "red-and-blue map of the culture wars"; in paragraph 3, where these attitudes are shown to differ from those of the general public; and in paragraph 6, where their attitudes are compared with those of previous generations. Since Hulbert is speculating on the basis of slim data, these passages pointing out how Gen Next differs from other groups in American society are needed to support her emerging thesis about what may make Gen Nexters unique. The strategy is not entirely convincing for this reason.

3. The comparison-contrast pattern is related to the strategy of negation since Hulbert is contrasting Gen Nexters with other groups such as liberals, conservatives, earlier generations, and the general public. She also contrasts "life-cycle effects" with "cohort effects." Words that signal comparison and contrast include the following: "Yet" (2); "By contrast," "compared with" (3); "But a more intriguing possibility," "Liberals…. Conservatives" (5); "On one level," "At the same time" (6); and "Judged against" (7).

4. The delayed thesis allows the reader to accompany Hulbert on her speculative musings about the significance of Gen Nexters' attitudes toward abortion and gay marriage. Since her thesis is quite hypothetical and impossible to support fully at this point in time, having it emerge by the end of the article is appropriate. The essay is essentially an exploratory piece and not a thesis-driven argument. On the other hand, some students may argue that the essay would be better if the thesis were stated at the beginning in order to forecast the essay's contents for the reader.

LIFE AS TYPE A

James Gleick

Questions for Close Reading (p. 385)

1. The thesis is clearly stated in the first sentence of paragraph 4: "We believe in Type A—a triumph for a notion with no particular scientific validity." Prior to paragraph 4, Gleick illustrates the cultural pervasiveness of the Type A category and traces its identification to Friedman and Rosenman's studies; these studies attempted to link heart disease to a set of personality traits clustered around the "theme of impatience" (paragraph 2). Following the statement of his thesis, Gleick challenges the scientific validity of Type A, while observing its compelling cultural relevance. He concludes the essay in paragraph 12 by reiterating the thesis; he says that linking the Type A phenomenon to cardiac problems "made for poor medical research," but "it stands nonetheless as a triumph of social criticism."

2. Friedman and Rosenman's study "Association of Specific Overt Behavior Pattern with Blood and Cardiovascular Findings" looked at connections between heart disease (including high blood pressure) and Type A behaviors. Gleick gives several reasons why the study was "obvious and false" and "a wildly flawed piece of research" (5). Readers can learn from his analysis how to evaluate the reliability of a study. First, *sample number*: Only a small number of people were studied. Group A consisted of only 83 people. Second, *types of subjects studied*: In this study, the subjects were all men. Third, *selection of subjects*: The research subjects were not chosen at random. Instead, Friedman and Rosenman selected subjects who shared similar professional and personal characteristics. They were generally "white-collar male employees of large businesses" (5) who exhibited stressed behavior, who smoked, and who were overweight. Fourth, *accounting for variables*: Rather than acknowledging these shared characteristics and the possibility that they might be

141

associated with heart disease, Friedman and Rosenman instead claimed that the Type A personality—rather than the subjects' unhealthy behaviors—was responsible for Group A's medical problems. Gleick also cites the researchers' amorphous definition of Type B as evidence of their flawed understanding of Type A.

3.   "The notion of Type A has expanded, shifted, and flexed to suit the varying needs of different researchers," writes Gleick in paragraph 7. He calls Type A a "grab-bag" of traits; researchers pick and choose those characteristics that reinforce their predetermined conclusions. Such researchers, each with a definite agenda, jump on the Type A bandwagon, producing sometimes alarming, sometimes ludicrous, but usually problematic results. For instance, researcher V.A. Price associated hypervigilance with the Type A personality. And researcher Cynthia Perry applied her interest in the study of daydreams to the Type A phenomenon and was able to conclude that Type As daydream less often than other people. Similarly, National Institutes of Health researchers looking at the effects of petless-ness on particular groups connected the incidence of heart disease in Type A people with the condition of petless-ness. Further, researchers interested in the behavior of children—even babies—have extended the reach of the phenomenon to include this group: babies who cry more are Type A (7).

     Gleick concludes that even before they begin their studies, these researchers already have in mind how Type A will be tied into their findings, and they manipulate the studies "until they find some correlation, somewhere . . ." (8). He concludes, "The categorizations are too variable and the prophecies too self-fulfilling" (9).

4.   Gleick demonstrates that the Type B personality has been "defined not by the personality traits its members possess but by the traits they lack" (10). He remarks somewhat disparagingly that Friedman and Rosenman were able to find only eighty men—municipal clerks and embalmers—"in all San Francisco" who, unlike Type A sufferers, did *not* feel that they were under any time constraints (10). The researchers labeled these men as having the Type B personality. Gleick implies that this identification by default of a small, nonrepresentative sample is further evidence of the researchers' unscientific practices. As the "shadowy opposites" of Type As, Type Bs, according to Gleick, "do *not* wear out their fingers punching the elevator button. They do *not* allow a slow car in the fast lane to drive their hearts to fatal distraction; in fact, they are at the wheel of the slow car" (10). In essence, Gleick implies that scientists' vague, amorphous definition of Type B reinforces the dubious scientific validity of Type A.

5. *coinage* (1): an invented word or phrase
    harrying (2): harassing, annoying
    canonical (2): authoritative, officially approved
    circuitously (2): indirectly
    sanctimoniously (4): hypocritically righteous
    overt (5): open, observable, not hidden
    incipient (5): beginning to exist or appear
    sedentary (6): inactive
    hypervigilance (7): excessive watchfulness
    correlation (8): mutual relation of two or more things
    strident (9): loud, harsh, grating, or shrill
    staccato (9): disjointed, abrupt
    foil (10): opposite
    totem (12): venerated emblem or symbol

Questions About the Writer's Craft (p. 386)

1. Although Gleick questions the scientific basis of Friedman and Rosenman's link between heart disease and Type A behavior, he seeks to show the universality of many of the Type A personality traits ascribed to Paul. Gleick counts on the fact that we've all met a Paul and could well have some of Paul in us. As Gleick goes on to argue, Paul's Type A personality is shaped not by personal psychology but by the society in which he lives—the same society that, to some extent, has engendered Type A traits in us all.

2. The three fragments—"Excessive competitiveness. Aggressiveness. 'A harrying sense of time urgency'"—are, according to Gleick, how Friedman and Rosenman describe the Type A personality. Gleick likely intended these choppy, clipped fragments to mimic the hurried, fast-paced lifestyle of the Type A person.

3. Gleick uses the personal pronouns "we," "us," and "our" throughout his essay. In the first paragraph of the essay, for instance, he asserts that Type A "is a token of our confusion" and asks, "[A]re we victims or perpetrators of the crime of haste? Are we living at high speed with athleticism and vigor, or are we stricken by hurry sickness?" These queries involve and hook us; they are *about* us; they cause us to want to read on. Because he knows that most readers will identify with these Type A characteristics, he seeks to show that Type A is less a medical condition than a cultural one. We are members of the society that has embraced the Type A phenomenon. We are Type A people because of the high-intensity society in which we live. It is also important to note that the pronouns "us," "we," and "our" include

143

Gleick himself; he, too, is a member of the society that has embraced and perpetuated the Type A lifestyle.

4. Gleick's sarcasm reflects his frustration and annoyance with the medical establishment's attempts to find scientific correlations where no valid ones exist. Other examples of sentences, phrases, and words that strike a similar tone include "standard medical knowledge untainted by research" (4); "cardiovascular comeuppance" (4); "the original Type A grab-bag" (7); "This is sweet, but it is not science" (7); "even more bizarrely" (11); and the last sentence of paragraph 11, which asserts, "No wonder they omitted Type C from the subsequent publicity." Considered together, these sentences and phrases establish the author's stance: one of bemused dismay, even disappointment, at the unscientific treatment the scientific community has given the Type A phenomenon.

SETTING THE RECORD STRAIGHT

Scott McCloud

Questions for Close Reading (p. 394)

1. McCloud states his thesis on page 2: "If people failed to understand comics, it was because they defined what comics could be too narrowly! A proper definition, if we could find one, might give lie to the stereotypes—and show that the potential of comics is limitless and exciting!"

2. The speaker identifies himself as a character named "Scott McCloud," the author of the book (1). This character is shown sitting in a studio, at a drawing board with a pencil in his hand. So he is clearly an artist. (In one frame on page 1, the reader can even see that the McCloud character is working on the very comic we are reading.) The speaker tells us that as a child he was not much interested in comics. But when he was introduced to comics in the eighth grade, he became "obsessed" (2) and began creating comics of his own. Slowly, he came to feel that comics had untapped "potential." He felt frustrated, though, because other people did not see the same potential he saw in comics. He decided to write about comics as a way of demonstrating what comics *could* be.

3. The author refers to Will Eisner, whom he describes as a "master comics artist." (Elsewhere in his book, McCloud mentions Eisner's *Comics and Sequential Art*;

Copyright © 2011, 2009, 2006, 2003 by Pearson Education, Inc.

some students may know Eisner and his work.) McCloud uses Eisner's description of comics as "sequential art" (3) as a starting point for his own definition. Quoting Eisner lets the reader know that comics can be a serious subject of study. It lends some legitimacy to McCloud's work.

4. McCloud says that he needs to "separate form from content" (3) to arrive at a definition. His series of definitions clearly deals with comics' form. McCloud proposes six definitions before arriving at his final version: "sequential art" (4), "sequential visual art" (4), "juxtaposed sequential visual art" (5), "juxtaposed sequential static images" (5), "juxtaposed static images in deliberate sequence" (5), and "juxtaposed pictorial and other images in deliberate sequence" (6). Each definition builds on the previous one, and the change in each is a response to a criticism about the previous definition. The final version is "juxtaposed pictorial and other images in deliberate sequence, intended to convey information and/or to produce an aesthetic response in the viewer" (6). The author has the McCloud character holding up a placard with each definition, so readers are easily able to identify each discrete definition.

5. *lurking* (page 2): waiting around in secret
   stereotypes (2): simplified or exaggerated ideas about a place, a group of people, or a thing
   transformed (3): changed in a major way
   neutral (3): neither good nor bad; not favoring any particular view of a matter
   aesthetic (3): artistic
   juxtaposed (4): adjacent; side-by-side
   arbitrary (5): random
   static (5): unmoving; still

Questions About the Writer's Craft (p. 394)

1. Defining comics in stages allows the author to build suspense for the reader. His technique also draws the reader in so that the reader feels like a participant in the definition activity. Finally, the stages approach is dramatic and seems to move forward. Giving the final version at the beginning and then explaining each term could, by contrast, seem static and pedantic. The evolution of a definition through stages emphasizes, as the definition expands, the points McCloud makes in his thesis—that the traditional definition is too narrow and that an ideal definition would allow for many possible uses of comics.

2.   Narration occurs in the story that starts and ends the reading. In that story, we encounter the McCloud character as an adult artist (1 and 6). In a flashback in that basic story, the McCloud character tells how his interest in comics developed (2). The narration's purpose is to show why the thesis is personally important to the author and to pique the reader's interest in the selection. We want to see how the author will define in a new way a term that we already feel we know quite well. The narrative is very effective in getting us engaged in the possibly dry activity of defining a term.

   In the middle of the reading, the author breaks away from the narrative to establish another scene—the McCloud character is now standing in a theater before an audience (4–6). At this point, the author employs argumentation to advance the definition. As each definition is proposed, a criticism or opposing viewpoint emerges from the "audience." The definition is then changed to address the criticism. In this way, the author sets up and answers one argument after another. This section also retains the feeling of a dramatic narrative because of the "theater" setting and because the criticisms are attributed to various "characters" in the scene. The ongoing dramatic quality keeps the reader engaged and wondering what will happen next.

3.   The author varies the sizes and shapes of frames to keep the selection from becoming predictable and, consequently, boring. Sometimes action happens without a frame, as at the bottom of page 1. In one case, the character breaks out of the frame—middle right column of page 6. Backgrounds are varied in darkness, and background scenes also vary. On page 5 (left) the author visually approximates a strip of film to make his point. Although there are a number of frames that show just the McCloud character speaking, the author is careful to vary those with other views and not to put too much text in any one frame. Finally, humorous details such as the row of obvious comic-book characters in the "audience" on page 4 reward the careful reader. Though his purpose is somewhat serious, the author maintains a lighthearted, even humorous tone throughout, using visual humor (for example, the ax on page 3) and verbal humor ("You tell 'im, Bob," on page 5).

4.   McCloud generally follows an English-language reader's natural inclination to read from left to right and from top to bottom. The frames are arranged in rows that basically read in those directions. In addition, McCloud uses some transitional signals—arrows pointing the reader in the right direction (3) and a change in basic background color from light in the narrative section to dark in the "theater" section. Also McCloud is careful when he shifts visual perspective so that readers will not be confused about who is talking to whom.

ANSWERS FOR CHAPTER 18
"ARGUMENTATION-PERSUASION" (p. 398)

OPENING COMMENTS

First-year composition courses often end with argumentation-persuasion. There are good reasons for this. Since an argumentation-persuasion essay can use a number of patterns of development, it makes sense to introduce this mode after students have had experience working with a variety of patterns. Also argumentation-persuasion demands logical reasoning and sensitivity to the nuances of language. We've found that earlier papers—causal analysis and comparison-contrast, for example—help students develop the reasoning and linguistic skills needed to tackle this final assignment.

When teaching argumentation-persuasion, we stress that the pattern makes special demands. Not only do writers have to generate convincing support for their positions, but they also must acknowledge and deal with opposing points of view. Having to contend with a contrary viewpoint challenges students to dig into their subjects so that they can defend their position with conviction. Students should find the material on pages 404–17 helpful; it illustrates different ways to acknowledge and refute the opposition.

Despite their initial moans and groans, students typically end up enjoying the challenge of argumentation-persuasion. To help students become more aware of the characteristics of this pattern of development, we often ask them to look through current newspapers and magazines and clip editorials and advertisements they find effective. In class, these items provide the basis for a lively discussion about the strategies unique to argumentation-persuasion. For example, the endorsement of a health club by a curvaceous television celebrity raises the issue of credibility, or *ethos*. An editorial filled with highly charged language ("We must unite to prevent this boa constrictor of a highway from strangling our neighborhood") focuses attention on the connotative power of words.

We often conclude our composition courses with an assignment based on a controversial issue. Depending on the time available and the skill of our students, the assignment may or may not require outside research. If it does call for research, we begin by having the class as a whole brainstorm as many controversial social issues as they can. Then for each issue the class generates a pair of propositions representing opposing viewpoints. Here are a few examples of what one of our classes came up with:

Controversial Subject	*Propositions*
School prayer	Prayer in public schools should/should not be allowed.
Drug abuse in professional sports	Professional sports should/should not implement a program of mandatory drug testing.
Adoption	Adopted children should/should not be given the means to contact their biological parents.

If the statement doesn't include research, we focus attention on more immediate local problems. Using the sequence just described, we start the activity by asking the class as a whole to brainstorm as many controversial campus problems as they can. Here are some argumentation-persuasion topics that have resulted.

Controversial Subject	*Propositions*
Cheating	A student found guilty of cheating should/should not be suspended.
Fraternities and sororities	Fraternities and sororities should/should not be banned from campus.
Drinking	The campus pub should/should not be licensed to serve liquor.

Once the propositions have been generated, the activity can go in one of two directions. We might ask students to pair up by issue, with the students in each pair taking opposing positions. Or we might have the students in each pair select the same position. Although students often end up qualifying their propositions, starting with a definitive thesis helps focus students' work in the early stages of the activity.

We try to schedule the assignment so that there is enough time for students to write their essays and deliver their arguments orally. The presentations take about one class; we call this class either "Forum on Contemporary Social Issues" or "Forum on Critical Campus Issues." Students tell us that they enjoy and learn a good deal from these brief oral presentations. (By the way, we grade only the papers, not the talks.)

We have been pleased by the way this final activity energizes students, pulling them out of the inevitable end-of-semester slump. The forum creates a kind of learning fellowship—not a bad way to end the course.

This chapter's professional readings illustrate the mix of logical support and emotional appeal characteristic of argumentation-persuasion. Quindlen ("Driving to the Funeral") asks what can be done to stop teens from dying in car accidents. To develop her assertion that the threat of failure should be regularly utilized to motivate students to work up to their potential, Sherry ("In Praise of the 'F' Word") relates her experiences as a teacher and a mother and thus establishes her *ethos* on the subject. Garibaldi ("How the Schools Shortchange Boys") discusses how teaching is geared toward the learning style of girls, leaving boys at a disadvantage, while Kimmel ("A War Against Boys?") says that if boys perform worse than girls in school other factors such as race and class may be at work. Rodriguez ("The Border on Our Backs") and Parker ("*Se Habla* Entitlement") both refer to racism and civil rights in establishing their opposing points of view.

ACTIVITIES: ARGUMENTATION-PERSUASION

Below we provide possible responses to selected activities at the end of Chapter 18. Of course, your students will devise their own inventive approaches.

Prewriting Activities (p. 429)

1. Listed below are some possible approaches to each of the topics. We recommend that you have students share their responses to this activity in groups or pairs. Seeing how others handled the assignments can provide inspiration for their own work.

    Topic: Defining hypocrisy

    Possible Audience: Employers
    Essay might argue the merit of these ways of behaving:

    Some employees react negatively to the hypocrisy of bosses not practicing what they preach. Employers should be careful to dispense advice that they themselves are willing to follow. For example, they shouldn't reprimand staff for taking office supplies if they also "borrow" such supplies; they shouldn't write memos outlawing personal phone calls if they themselves make such calls.

    Topic: The difference between license and freedom

    Possible Audience: College students
    Essay might argue the merit of these ways of behaving:

149

While license involves nothing more than indulging one's every whim, freedom means acting with thoughtful regard for consequences. Students, then, should think before going out to party before an exam, should reconsider substituting an easy course for a difficult one, and so on.

2. Here are the audience analyses for each thesis:

    a. Low-income employees: Supportive
        Employers: Hostile
        Congressional representatives: Wavering

    b. College students: Hostile
        Parents: Wavering or hostile
        College officials: Wavering or supportive

    c. Environmentalists: Supportive
        Homeowners: Hostile
        Town council members: Wavering

Revising Activities (p. 430)

6. a. *Implied warrant:* Strict quality control is necessary to produce cars that have superior fuel efficiency and longevity.

        This warrant is clearly implied and probably does not need to be stated explicitly. The warrant does not need additional support, nor does the claim need qualification. The writer might, however, add more specific data to the argument.

    b. *Implied warrant:* Gifted children require special educational programs, just as do the learning impaired.

        This warrant should be made explicit, and it should be backed up with additional data that proves that gifted children need special programs. The claim might also be qualified to state that "sometimes" or "often" the educational system is unfair to the gifted.

    c. *Implied warrant:* Prejudice plays a major role in determining how citizens vote for president.

This warrant should be made explicit; additional data should be provided to show that prejudice has actually influenced voters' behavior in specific contests.

7. a. ***Inductive reasoning,*** moving from the events in the computer lab to a general conclusion. The conclusion is invalid because there may be other causes of the problems in the lab; for example, perhaps the support staff needs better training or perhaps the writer needs further instruction in the use of the programs.

   b. ***Inductive reasoning,*** moving from the evidence of the dented cars to a general conclusion. The conclusion is invalid because there may be many reasons for the dents in the cars. For example, perhaps many students cannot afford new cars and thus drive used cars that were dented by previous owners.

   c. ***Deductive reasoning,*** applying a general true statement about the qualities shown by children of two-career families to a particular situation—specifically, that of the increase of such families in a nearby town. This conclusion is invalid because the conclusion is much broader than the evidence supports. It would be more valid to say that "Some children" or "More children than ever" in the nearby town are likely to develop confidence and independence.

8. a. ***Begging the Question.*** The statement that "Grades are irrelevant to learning" requires proof, but this argument skips over this debatable premise. The second statement is also debatable; some students, those wishing to attend graduate school, for example, are in college to "get good grades."

   b. ***Overgeneralization; Either-Or; Begging the Question.*** Both statements are debatable; for example, that jail provides a "taste of reality" is questionable, and that juvenile offenders will repeat crimes "over and over" unless jailed needs to be proven. Moreover, the argument presents only two alternatives: "either" a juvenile offender is jailed "or" the offender will repeat crimes. It is possible to imagine other outcomes from not jailing juvenile offenders: With therapy, community service, job training, or suspended sentences, some may "go straight"; others may commit different crimes instead of "repeating" their initial crimes.

   c. ***Overgeneralization; Begging the Question; Card Stacking.*** The first statement in this argument is an overly general description of the programs: They "do nothing to decrease the rate of teenage pregnancy." In addition, the argument

151

begs the question of whether the programs truly fail to curtail teen pregnancies. The argument also fails to address whether there are other valuable accomplishments of the programs that might make them worth keeping. (For example, such programs most likely help reduce instances of sexually transmitted diseases.) Finally, the phrase "so-called sex education programs" is also a way of card stacking; this term denigrates the programs without saying what's wrong with them.

d. ***Either-Or; Card Stacking.*** This argument admits of only two possibilities; "either" our country should use coal "or" become "enslaved" to the countries that sell oil. In reality, there are many more options, including developing other fuel sources such as solar, wind, or water power and increasing our ability to find, recover, and process oil in our own country. In addition, the use of the highly connotative word "enslaved" stacks the cards by predisposing people toward unthinking agreement with the argument.

e. ***False Analogy; Non Sequitur.*** By likening abortion to killing the homeless and pulling the plug on sick people, this argument commits a false analogy. In reality, these are all quite different situations with differing moral issues, motivations, and outcomes. Secondly, it is a non sequitur to assume that if abortion is permitted that people "will think it's acceptable" to commit the other actions mentioned. There's actually no demonstrated causal connection between society's permitting abortion and its accepting the murder of unfortunate people.

f. ***Ad Hominem.*** This argument attacks the background of those who support gun control instead of dismantling the arguments for their position; it attempts to destroy the credibility of those who hold the anti-gun point of view. In fact, even if the credibility of the anti-gun legislators were negligible, there still may be valid reasons for supporting their point of view.

9. It's a good idea to set aside some time for students to see how others went about revising this paragraph. They may discover options they hadn't considered.

Here are some of the problems with the introduction:

— Throughout the paragraph there's a hostile, confrontational tone that undercuts the impact of the position being advanced. Sarcastic descriptions of the administrators amount to an *ad hominem* attack: "acting like fascists" and "in their supposed wisdom" (both in sentence 2) and "somehow or another they got it into their heads" (sentence 5). These accusatory descriptions of the way the administration came to impose the dress code should be replaced with a more realistic explanation of why they made the decision they did. A more objective tone is called for.

— Inflammatory language used in the first two sentences stacks the cards in favor of the writer's point of view: "outrageously strong," "issued an edict," "preposterous dress code." Similar card stacking occurs in the fourth sentence when the writer refers to the administrators' "dictatorial prohibition." Such phrases need to be replaced by more neutral language.

— The writer's point that students will lose their "constitutional rights" (sentence 2) is not substantiated in any way. A brief explanation of this point would be appropriate.

— The statement (sentence 3) that "Perhaps the next thing they'll want to do is forbid students to play rock music at school dances" is a non sequitur; instituting a dress code has no causal relationship to restricting music at school dances. This statement might also be considered a red herring because it brings in an unrelated issue about which the reader might have strong feelings. In any case, this unfounded prediction should be eliminated.

— There is no sound basis for the recommendation (sentence 6) that students and parents should protest all dress codes. Any such recommendation should be reserved for the end of the essay, after a logical, well-reasoned argument has been advanced. At that point, it would be appropriate to name specific actions parents could take, such as calling the principal or speaking out at a PTA meeting.

— The final statement that if dress codes are implemented "we might as well throw out the Constitution" embodies at least two fallacies. It is an either-or statement admitting of no lesser or even other consequences. It also is a non sequitur, because no cause-effect relationship has been shown to exist between dress codes and the end of constitutional rights. This closing statement should be eliminated.

— Finally, the paragraph uses the cause-effect pattern but presents no evidence for the causal relationship it claims. The writer discounts the causes of the administrators' decision (the current dress habits of the student body) and predicts extreme and unsubstantiated effects of the dress code. In revising, students might choose some of the following options: dispute the administration's claims that the lack of a dress code creates problems, discuss

153

other possible ways of handling these problems, or analyze possible negative effects of a dress code. Of course, not all of these options could be pursued in the introductory paragraph, but they point the way to possible strategies for developing the rest of the essay in a thoughtful, logical manner.

DRIVING TO THE FUNERAL

Anna Quindlen

Questions for Close Reading (p. 434)

1. Quindlen's thesis emerges slowly in this article. Paragraph 1 introduces the issue by describing a teenager's funeral and stating, "It's become a sad rite of passage in many American communities, the services held for teenagers killed in auto accidents before they've even scored a tassel to hang from the rearview mirror." From that point on, Quindlen explores the measures that have been taken to prevent teen driving accidents and why they have not worked, eventually stating her thesis and call to action in the eighth paragraph: "States might make it easier on themselves, on police officers and on teenagers, too, if instead of chipping away at the right to drive they merely raised the legal driving age wholesale."

2. Quindlen discusses two solutions to the problem of teen auto accidents that she claims have not worked. The first is raising the drinking age to 21 (paragraphs 4, 5). Although the number of traffic fatalities has fallen since 1984, when the age was raised, Quindlen indicates that it is not clear that the higher drinking age caused this reduction. According to her, improved auto-safety features like seat belts and air bags may be primarily responsible for the reduction in fatalities. The second solution to the problem is the provisional license, which restricts the driving freedoms of the youngest drivers (6, 7). Quindlen acknowledges this is a good idea but claims that the provisions are not enforced, so that the provisional license is "toothless" (7).

3. According to Quindlen, in Europe governments do not focus on the drinking age. Instead, they are strict with the provisions of their driver's licenses, and in most countries the legal driving age is 18 (5).

4. Quindlen favors dispensing with provisional licenses and raising the legal driving age across the board. She doesn't indicate what age would be suitable, however. One can infer from the article that the age would be 17 or 18 rather than 16. Note that

154

Quindlen's position on this issue is influenced by her residence in New York City, where public transportation is a viable alternative to driving.

5. *inexorably* (1): relentlessly, unable to be stopped
posthumously (1): after death
inalienable (2): incapable of being surrendered or given up
exurb (3): a region beyond a city and its suburbs
roundelay (3): a poem or song with a frequently recurring refrain
neophyte (3): novice, beginner
sanctioned (4): officially approved or permitted
provisional (7): serving for the time being
untenable (8): not able to be defended

Questions About the Writer's Craft (p. 436)

1. Quindlen seems to have geared her argument for a hostile audience. In fact, there are several criticisms of members of her audience in the article, specifically adults with children. In paragraphs 2 and 3, she accuses parents of being passive about the driving problem and valuing their own convenience over their children's safety. She repeats this claim in her final paragraph: "Lots and lots of parents will tell you that raising the driving age is untenable, that the kids need their freedom and their mobility." These criticisms may put many of her readers on the defensive rather than rallying them to Quindlen's cause.

2. Quindlen's statistics are relevant, unified, and specific, supporting her thesis. They are also dramatic, representative, and, as far as we know, accurate. Since the essay follows the conventions of journalism, however, the statistics are not thoroughly documented, and in fact most are even presented without attribution. Her citation of the National Highway Traffic Safety Administration (3) to support the claim that even 17-year-olds have considerably lower accident rates than 16-year-olds encourages the reader to feel that all the statistics are probably accurate and representative. However, it's difficult to tell for sure. Those statistics presented without attribution include car crashes being the number one cause of death among 15- to 20-year-olds (2), the decrease in fatalities from 1984 to the present (4), survey results (5), the increase in the chance of an accident when two or more teens are passengers (6), the number of tickets to provisional drivers (7), and the accident rate of 16-year-olds (8). For this reason, the statistical support of the argument is not adequate, a flaw common in magazine and newspaper opinion pieces.

3. Quindlen uses a description of a teenager's funeral in the first paragraph to introduce the issue of teen traffic fatalities and to hook the reader. She also uses cause and effect to explain why in her view the two solutions to teen accidents are not working. The first, raising the drinking age to 21, cannot definitively be said to be the cause of reduced traffic fatalities since 1984, according to Quindlen, since improved auto-safety features may be the primary cause. The second, giving younger drivers provisional licenses, has not had the intended effect since, according to Quindlen, police do not enforce the terms of these licenses.

4. The main appeals to *pathos* in this essay are in the introduction and the conclusion. In the first paragraph, Quindlen describes a teen's funeral and the emotions it evokes in the victim's friends and family. This is a powerful emotional introduction to the issue. In the body of the essay Quindlen focuses mostly on *logos*, although there is one appeal to *pathos*. In paragraph 7 she describes a particular deadly accident, which puts a human face on the statistics she has been citing. Finally, in the concluding sentences Quindlen evokes the grief and remorse of parents of teens who have died in auto accidents. This conclusion buttresses her call for action at the start of the last paragraph.

IN PRAISE OF THE "F" WORD

Mary Sherry

Questions for Close Reading (p. 439)

1. Sherry's thesis, implied, is a combination of the assertions she makes in paragraphs 2 and 4. In paragraph 2, after describing what brings students to adult literacy programs, she tells us that the real reason they wind up there is that "they have been cheated by our education system." She rounds out this point in paragraph 4 when she asserts that poor academic skills are less a result of "drugs, divorce, and other impediments" than they are a result of teachers' unwillingness to use the threat of failure as a motivating tool. Bringing these two points together, one may state Sherry's thesis as follows: Students are cheated by an educational system that refuses to make the possibility of failure a reality.

2. Deliberately shocking, this statement gains our attention immediately. Most of us should be appalled that so many students—tens of thousands—will receive diplomas that mean nothing. We wonder how such a thing could occur. But we also wonder

what Sherry means by the term "meaningless." Later in the essay, this question is answered. Meaningless diplomas have no substance. They are useless slips of paper for those students who have been ushered through to graduation despite the fact that they have failed to achieve passing grades. Sherry concludes that passing students along in this manner cheats them in a sort of slippery-slope way. To begin, they feel increasingly inadequate as they move to higher levels without having mastered the material meant to prepare them for more advanced subject matter. Some continue on in this manner, realizing only later how little they really have learned—their lack of skill resulting, among other things, in limited job opportunities or disgruntled employers. For others, failure becomes a state of mind. Never imagining they have the power to learn and thus to move ahead, they abandon the idea of learning altogether.

3. According to Sherry, educators don't give reasons for passing students with poor achievement records; educators make excuses instead. For instance, they say "kids can't learn if they come from terrible environments" (8) or have experienced such things as "unemployment, chemical dependency, abusive relationships" (9). In other words, neither teacher nor student is responsible for achievement, or the lack thereof; the world-at-large is responsible.

   What excuses like this amount to is a "Why bother?" attitude, which is particularly destructive because it results in a kind of self-fulfilling prophecy: If little is expected from students, there is little incentive for either teachers or students to work hard. Such a cavalier view of students' ability to succeed falls short of addressing what Sherry sees as the real problem: the dearth of incentive in education today. She writes, "No one seems to stop to think that—no matter what environments they come from—most kids don't put school first on their list unless they perceive something is at stake. They'd rather be sailing" (8). It is not that students can't be educated but that students are not encouraged to see education as necessary to their future success, something ultimately worth their time and energy.

4. Regardless of distractions, be they home life or peer related, in order to get students to concentrate teachers must gain students' attention. Most educators would agree that this is often easier said than done. And Sherry doesn't provide any specifics as to how this might be accomplished other than to say that teaching style has much to do with it (4). Since most instructors would rather not resort to turning cartwheels to keep students focused, Sherry gives another option when "style alone won't do it." She writes that "there is another way to show who holds the winning hand in the classroom. That is to reveal the trump card of failure." In other words, acrobatics are not necessary to move students to concentrate. What is needed is a clarification of the road to success: stay focused on schoolwork, or fail.

157

Adult students, having the wisdom that comes with experience, understand the importance of education, Sherry tells us. Often their livelihood depends upon success in the classroom this time around. Thus, what lies at the heart of their motivation is "a healthy fear of failure" (9). And this—the understanding that something is at stake—can and must, Sherry believes, be instilled in all students.

5. *validity* (1): soundness, effectiveness
   semiliterate (1): partially educated
   equivalency (2): equal to in value
   impediments (4): hindrances, obstructions
   composure (6): calmness and self-possession
   radical (6): extreme, revolutionary
   priority (6): of utmost importance
   resentful (7): angry or bitter about
   testimony (9): public declaration
   motivate (10): stir to action
   merit (11): value
   conspiracy (11): plot
   illiteracy (11): having little or no formal education, esp. the inability to read and write

Questions About the Writer's Craft (p. 440)

1. To convince readers that she knows of what she speaks, Sherry establishes her qualifications early on. She tells us in the first sentence of paragraph 2 that many of the students awarded meaningless diplomas eventually find their way into adult literacy programs such as the one where she teaches basic grammar and writing. In other words, as an adult-literacy teacher, she knows firsthand the type of student she refers to in the selection. Moreover, as we learn in paragraph 3, her experience as an educator has taught her "a lot about our schools." And what she has learned, as her examples make clear, directly relates to the issue of passing students through the system regardless of achievement. But Sherry doesn't stop there. To make sure her audience does not lose sight of her credibility, throughout the essay she refers either to herself as a teacher or to her teaching experiences (paragraphs 4, 7, 9).

   Still, being a teacher is not the sum of Sherry's qualifications. Her home-life credentials her further. She is the parent of a student whose teacher used the "trump card of failure" to get him to succeed. Identifying herself at the outset and establishing her qualifications so often (and in more than one way) indicate that Sherry anticipates a possibly skeptical audience—one that requires a knowledgeable and credentialed voice if they are going to consider what she has to say, much less be led to her way of thinking.

2. The title probably makes readers think of a well-known scatological term. And Sherry probably hoped for this effect, for as outlandish as it seems, we might then assume she is going to argue the attributes of this term and its usage. This thought alone is likely to arouse readers' curiosity; they will want to read on to find out why Sherry applauds the F-word. This is probably why Sherry chose this play on words for a title. Through it, she gets our attention.

3. Sherry quotes her students in paragraphs 3 and 7. By using these direct quotations, Sherry lets us experience directly how these students feel about their educational experiences and their own abilities. Through their words, Sherry demonstrates that the problem she sees is very real. She has come to understand the problem by listening to the statements she now shares with us. The students' direct testimony is her most valid proof that a problem exists. Although Sherry articulates the issue and argues the point, her students' comments illustrate that there is no one better than the students themselves to convey the reality of the problem.

4. Sherry's main proof that the threat of failure can work comes in the form of a personal example. We learn that although nothing could move Sherry's son before, he was motivated to succeed in his English class by the threat of flunking (5–6). Although Sherry concedes that one piece of proof is hardly enough—"I know one example doesn't make a case" (7)—this one example helps her support her position in a number of ways. To begin, using a personal example brings her readers closer to her and thus closer to her subject matter. In addition, this particular example has special power because it consists of a parent, a student, a teacher: There is someone in the example for almost any reader to identify with. Parents can imagine themselves in Sherry's shoes, having to accept that the threat of failure is the best way to motivate their child. Teachers can envision themselves as Mrs. Stifter, adhering to an unpopular policy because it brings about the hoped-for results. And students can ally themselves with Sherry's son, a boy who chooses to succeed when the only alternative is to fail.

HOW THE SCHOOLS SHORTCHANGE BOYS

Gerry Garibaldi

Questions for Close Reading (p. 445)

1. Garibaldi states his thesis in the first and second paragraphs. The first paragraph is just one brief sentence ("In the newly feminized classroom, boys tune out."), and the second paragraph elaborates on this sentence by citing the work of Christina Hoff Sommers. Her book *The War Against Boys* claims that in making schools more girl-friendly at the behest of feminists, educators have harmed boys.

2. According to Garibaldi, males react to an assignment by questioning its point: "They want a rational explanation for everything" (13). This is illustrated by Brandon's questioning a social-studies assignment and being given detention by his teacher, who objected to the rudeness of his question (9), and by the reluctance of the author and a male colleague to participate in a mixed-group workshop on heterogeneous grouping in the classroom (16). In contrast, according to Garibaldi, female students, who value cooperation, "obediently flip their notebooks open" (12), and adult females value the social goal of equality (19).

3. According to Garibaldi, so many boys are tested for disabilities because boys don't flourish in the "feminized" classroom. Elementary-school teachers, who are mostly women, value obedience and classroom order; they "tend to view boys' penchant for challenging classroom assignments as disruptive" (14). Parents are looking for a solution to their son's performance in school—"his poor self-esteem and unhappiness, his discipline problems" (22)—and they see special education as an opportunity to get academic benefits for their children even though "it's all a hustle" (22). The catch is that students must be diagnosed with a disability in order to qualify for special education, and this has a negative psychological effect on students (23).

4. Garibaldi's student Brandon essentially games the special-ed system. He "knows his legal rights as well as his caseworkers do" (29), and he insists on them to the letter (31). As a consequence, according to Garibaldi, his own position as a teacher is undermined (32), while Brandon's attention is focused on the "process of education" (33) rather than its content.

5. *pernicious* (1): destructive
   disengaged (2): detached

160

rationalist (4): relying on reason
precocious (11): mature for one's age
bane (11): source of harm; curse
penchant (14): inclination or liking
inimical (14): hostile
predilection (15): a strong preference
heterogeneous (15): mixed
cohort (16): colleague
contentious (19): having a tendency to quarrels and disputes
irreducible (20): impossible to make less or smaller
plummet (23): to drop sharply
motes (26): small particles
withering (33): devastating
rectitude (33): righteousness
pander (34): to gratify the desires of others
resiliency (45): (alt. of *resilience*) the ability to recover easily

Questions About the Writer's Craft (p. 445)

1. Garibaldi starts off with expert testimony by quoting Christina Hoff Sommers's book *The War Against Boys* (paragraphs 2, 4) and with some statistics about the educational achievements of boys and girls (3). For these statistics, he cites "education researcher" Jay Greene, although he does not give sufficient source information for readers to verify the research. But expert testimony and statistics occur in only 4 of 44 paragraphs. The main evidence is from Garibaldi's personal observation and experience as a teacher, as illustrated by the extended example of special-ed student Brandon, the teacher's seminar on heterogeneous grouping in the classroom, and school-textbook illustrations. Since the preponderance of the evidence is anecdotal and based on the author's limited experience, the evidence has a mixed effect. It simultaneously weakens the *logos* (soundness) of the argument while strengthening its *pathos* (emotional power).

2. Cause-effect is the basic pattern of the argument; the author uses it to further his claim that the "feminization" of the classroom has led to boys' dysfunction in school and the growth of special education (1–4, 11, 14, 20–23, 33). Garibaldi uses the comparison-contrast pattern to support the argument, by comparing boys' and girls' educational achievements, values, and behaviors (3, 12–21). He uses the process pattern to explain how special education works (22–28). Students may note two other major patterns as well: exemplification (the examples of Brandon and the teacher's seminar) and narrative (the Brandon stories).

161

3. Garibaldi uses strongly worded declarative statements elsewhere throughout the essay, in particular in the 2nd paragraph ("Sommers was absolutely accurate"), the 4th paragraph ("they don't want to be girls"), the 12th paragraph ("Teachers love them. God loves them. Girls are calm and pleasant. They succeed through cooperation"), the 21st paragraph ("the notion of male ethical inferiority"; "females diagnosed with learning disabilities simply don't exist"), and the 34th paragraph ("both women are second raters at best"). These phrases and sentences give the argument force and urgency, and for those who already agree with Garibaldi they are probably very effective. On the other hand, the language would tend to alienate people who oppose his argument, since their point of view is not acknowledged at all. In addition, the broad condemnation of feminism is likely to offend many women, even those who might not have a position on this issue. Thus the strong language prevents Garibaldi from establishing common ground and goodwill with a good portion of his readership.

4. Garibaldi uses vulgar and offensive language in the dialogue and quotations of real speech (9, 13, 18, 42). This gives the speech a lifelike quality, but it does nothing to advance Garibaldi's argument. It is simply realistic.

A WAR AGAINST BOYS?

Michael Kimmel

Questions for Close Reading (p. 452)

1. Kimmel's thesis is stated explicitly in paragraph 26: "It is not the school experience that 'feminizes' boys, but rather the ideology of traditional masculinity that keeps boys from wanting to succeed." The thesis statement is preceded by a methodical presentation of the facts, the opposing argument, and a rebuttal of each point of the opposing argument.

2. Kimmel mentions the college-enrollment statistics in paragraph 5. In paragraphs 12–14, he explains that the statistics typically cited to show that more girls than boys are going to college (5) are misleading because they are usually cited without reference to the past, to the numbers at elite colleges and universities, and to class and race. For example, he shows that although more girls than boys go to college, the rate of college attendance is increasing for both groups (12). Many of the highly ranked colleges and universities still enroll more men than women (13). Finally, among

working-class and black college students, there is indeed a great imbalance, with more women than men attending college. From this Kimmel concludes that the overall imbalance between the sexes in college has more to do with class and race than it does with gender.

3. In paragraphs 18 and 19, Kimmel describes the effect of adolescence on the behavior of girls and boys. For girls, adolescence is a time to "lose their voices" (Gilligan, quoted in paragraph 18) and "suppress their ambitions" (19). In contrast, during adolescence boys become more confident, adopting a false bravado (18), becoming more ambitious, and overvaluing their abilities (19).

4. By "the boy code" Kimmel means the posturing that males adopt during their teen years to prove their strength and assert their power. It involves "foolish risk-taking, and gratuitous violence" (18). It also leads them to overvalue their abilities and remain in programs even though they are less likely to succeed at them. Kimmel attributes much of teen boys' lower academic achievement to the boy code, which he also calls "the ideology of traditional masculinity" (26).

5. *docility* (2): the quality of being easily led or managed
    parse (3): to examine minutely
    bastion (5): stronghold
    par (5): equal
    pathologized (8): viewed as medically or psychologically diseased
    indolence (9): laziness
    sedentary (9): not physically active
    halcyon (10): peaceful, happy
    deportment (10): behavior
    rambunctious (10): unruly
    zero-sum (11): describing an activity in which a gain for one side results in a corresponding loss for the other
    putative (11): supposed, assumed to exist
    facile (15): simplistic, easy
    biologism (16): the use of biological explanations for social behaviors
    tautologies (17): needless repetitions
    anachronistic (27): out of place in time

Questions About the Writer's Craft (p. 452)

1. Kimmel starts his essay with an example of a high-school boy who is an average student but who is suing his school district for sex discrimination, claiming that

163

schools "routinely discriminate against males" (paragraph 2). The opening is effective in that anecdotes about specific people usually are more interesting and inviting to readers than more abstract introductions. It also helps to show that the issue of boys and education is being taken to extremes—even to the courts.

2. Kimmel cites the following experts who oppose his point of view: Tom Mortensen (5); Christina Hoff Sommers (8); Michael Gurian, author of *The Wonder of Boys* (8); and George Gilder, a writer for the *National Review* (8). In support of his point of view, Kimmel cites Michael Thompson and Dan Kindlon, authors of *Raising Cain* (17); Carol Gilligan (18); the researcher Wayne Martino (21); and Catharine Stimpson (21). The large number of experts cited—both pro and con—lead the reader to feel that the article is well researched and that the author is at pains to present both sides of this complex issue.

3. The cause-effect pattern is the main pattern used in this argument, as it is in the Garibaldi argument. In his essay, starting with paragraph 10, Kimmel tries to show that feminism is not the cause of boys' present educational status but that other factors are. Among them are the federal No Child Left Behind program, which has led to inadequate funding and cuts in gym, recess, and athletic programs that benefit boys (11); the greater incentives working-class and black women have to go to college (14); and the "ideology of masculinity," which pressures boys to behave in counterproductive ways (18–26).

4. According to the biographical note, Kimmel is a professor of sociology and a leading expert on the topic of men and masculinity in the United States. This background gives him a strong and credible *ethos* in two ways. First, his basic credentials as a sociology professor suggest that the evidence he cites in his argument is well researched and broad based (in contrast to Garibaldi, who relies heavily on personal observation and experience). Second, his subject-matter expertise on men in society means he comes to the issue with a great deal of background knowledge and insight that allows him to develop an argument with great breadth as well as depth. Students may disagree on how Kimmel's credentials influence their own reading of his argument. Some may value his academic expertise; others may think that his pro-feminist point of view leads him to ignore aspects of this issue.

THE BORDER ON OUR BACKS

Roberto Rodriguez

Questions for Close Reading (p. 456)

1. Rodriguez's thesis is dispersed throughout the essay. It could be stated as follows: "American sentiment against illegal immigrants from Mexico and Central America has deep racist roots, and these immigrants have a legitimate claim to be anywhere on the continent of North America, since their ancestors lived there."

2. The title, "The Border on Our Backs," means that immigrants set the borders in North America, not white politicians who draw arbitrary national boundaries on a map. In paragraph 10, Rodriguez describes the migrations of the ancestors of present-day immigrants as covering the whole continent. Therefore, according to Rodriguez, Mexican and Central American immigrants are at home wherever they are: "If anything, we are back."

   Another interpretation of the title is that immigrants are constantly burdened by questions of immigration and border integrity—in a sense, this is a cross they must constantly bear.

3. According to Rodriguez, American policies on immigration set up a "two-tiered society" of legal and illegal human beings. This is similar to apartheid, a policy of legalized segregation and political and economic discrimination against peoples of non-European ancestry that used to be the law in South Africa.

4. Rodriguez thinks that African Americans, Indian Americans, and other disadvantaged American subgroups should be the inspiration for illegal Mexican and Central American immigrants. That's because these groups provide a model for how to fight for and attain civil rights in U.S. society.

5. *scapegoats* (1): those who take the blame for the sins of others
   draconian (3): cruel, severe
   repatriations (3): sending people back to their country of origin
   apartheid (3): a system of legalized racial segregation in South Africa
   bigotry (6): intolerance for the beliefs and practices of others
   dragnet (6): a network of measures
   vilification (6): defamation, slander
   delude (7): to deceive
   indigenous (9): native

obliterated (9): wiped out
traversed (10): went from one end to another; crossed
amnesty (10): a general pardon
remanded (10): sent back
complicit (10): associated in wrongdoing

Questions About the Writer's Craft (p. 456)

1. The so-called U.S. political dictionary is of course nonexistent; these definitions are Rodriguez's way of provocatively stating the opposition's perspective and establishing his point of view. The idea that these definitions are from a U.S. political dictionary suggests that all Americans hold these views of Mexicans and Central Americans, a suggestion that many Americans would find offensive. The definitions themselves are exaggerated and ironic, which sets the tone for the remainder of the essay. This use of hyperbole is double-edged. On the one hand, it can engage readers who are already likely to sympathize with Rodriguez's point of view, but on the other hand it can alienate readers who may find themselves unfairly rendered here.

2. In paragraph 6, Rodriguez supports his claim that American attitudes toward Mexican and Central American immigrants are fundamentally racist by citing racial profiling of individuals at borders, immigrant raids that target "brown peoples," and the focus on the southern border with Mexico rather than the northern border with Canada. He presents each of these as a rhetorical question, the answer to which he considers self-evident. The evidence, as such, is not concrete. He is appealing more to *pathos* than to *logos* here.

3. The Mexican and Nahuatl expressions serve several purposes. First, they help to establish Rodriguez's credibility as a spokesman for illegal immigrants from Mexico and Central America; clearly, he has an intimate knowledge of their world, down to idiomatic and indigenous expressions. Second, some of them, like *migra* and *nopal*, are vivid expressions that give color and interest to the writing. Third, they serve to include some readers and exclude others since they are used mostly without translation. This actually suggests that Rodriguez is not targeting a general American audience but instead is expecting that his essay will be read mostly by people with a Hispanic background.

4. The main fallacy in this argument is a "begging the question" fallacy. Rodriguez fails to support his claim that Mexican and Central American immigrants have a right to be anywhere in North America. The fact that their ancestors may have moved freely around the continent in the past (if indeed that is true) doesn't mean that present-day

166

immigrants have the same right. Political systems of organization are different today, and national borders are significant barriers to migration throughout the world.

SE HABLA ENTITLEMENT

Star Parker

Questions for Close Reading (p. 460)

1. Parker states her thesis in the fourth paragraph: "I don't buy that, along with life, liberty and the pursuit of happiness, our Creator endowed anyone with the right to sneak into the United States, bypass our laws and set up shop."

2. Parker objects to immigration advocates adopting the strategies of the civil-rights movement, because the civil-rights movement was about "enforcing the law, not breaking it" (7). According to Parker, the movement focused on getting enforcement of existing laws (the post-Civil War constitutional amendments that granted rights to freed slaves). In addition, she points out that Mexicans do not seem to find it necessary to demonstrate for and demand the benefits of a free society in Mexico, where they do have rights, but do become politically active in the United States, where they don't have rights.

3. Parker attributes the increase in the size of the federal government to the large immigrant population of the United States. According to Parker, these immigrants make demands on taxpayers' money by needing schools, health care, law enforcement, and other government services, thereby perpetuating the welfare state.

4. Parker objects to the feeling of entitlement that she claims immigrants have, because in fact illegal immigrants have no legal standing here and thus no rights, especially not the rights of citizens. According to Parker, illegal immigrants are entitled to nothing in the United States.

5. *entitlement* (title): a right to benefits, especially those specified by law
   libertarian (1): a person who believes in the principle of liberty
   conundrum (1): a kind of riddle
   inalienable (3): not to be removed or transferred
   provoke (4): to make angry, to irritate
   bogus (6): false

167

garb (6): clothing
paragon (14): a model of perfection

Questions About the Writer's Craft (p. 460)

1. Parker uses the second strategy for refuting opposing points. She starts with her proposition (paragraphs 1–4); cites an opposing view in paragraphs 5, 10, 13; and refutes these points in paragraphs 7–9, 11–12, and 14. She then concludes with additional evidence supporting her argument (the burden immigrants place on government resources) in paragraphs 15 and 16.

    The first opposing view is that immigrants have a right to be here; she refutes this by saying that immigrants snuck into the country, breaking laws, and have no rights as a consequence.

    The second opposing view is that Mexicans would prefer to live in the United States because of the economic opportunities here. She uses research to cast doubt on this argument, first quoting a Pew Hispanic Center survey of adults in Mexico to establish the proof that 46 percent of adult Mexicans say they would prefer to live in the United States and then citing poll results favoring a leftist candidate for the Mexican presidency. She concludes that if Mexicans coming to the United States favored economic expansion, they would not support leftist political candidates whose policies do not.

    The third opposing view is that the Latino immigrant community simply wants to be free to work and maintain traditional families. Parker refutes this by citing crime, high dropout rates, and out-of-wedlock births in the Latino community in Southern California.

    Finally, she claims that immigrants tax the resources of the United States by demanding services.

    Students might argue that each of Parker's refutations is effective, in part because she keeps the discussion narrowly focused. She reinforces her argument with relevant statistics, and she does not raise issues that might undermine her argument. For example, she doesn't discuss the huge economic contribution of immigrant labor to the U.S. economy, or social-justice issues such as children's right to an education, or immigration policies that break up families when some members are deported.

    Students might also argue that Parker's refutations are ineffective. They might point out that the Pew statistics and polling results do not necessarily lead to a meaningful conclusion. Mexicans might favor a particular candidate for reasons other than his economic policy. She also glosses over important counterarguments—for example, that a major reason illegal immigrants sneak over the border is that

American businesses are eager to hire them and that most members of the Latino community are law-abiding.

2. Parker compares and contrasts the Latino and black communities of Southern California in order to show that the Latino community has as many problems with poverty as the black community. The problems she cites undermine the traditional family values that immigrants supposedly espouse. According to Parker, they serve to show that the immigrant community is not a desirable addition to the United States.

3. Parker's use of words and phrases from the Declaration of Independence serves to establish her *ethos* as a patriot whose principles are derived from one of the United States' most important and revered documents. These inalienable human rights do not include illegal immigration, which is lawbreaking, according to Parker. By using these words, Parker sets herself up alongside the Founding Fathers and in opposition to those who are not U.S. citizens.

4. The language indicating Parker's emotions and reactions helps establish her as an ordinary person with deep-seated responses to the immigration issue. These words and phrases create a link to the reader, who can recognize her humanity in her reactions. This appeal to *pathos* makes Parker's argument stronger than if she had merely relied on logic to refute the positions of pro-immigrant groups.

ANSWERS FOR CHAPTER 19
"LOCATING, EVALUATING, AND INTEGRATING RESEARCH SOURCES"

[Full and Brief versions only;
this chapter does not appear in the Concise Edition]

Below we provide possible responses to selected activities at the end of Chapter 19. We hope these suggested responses convey the range of answers possible.

1. Here are possible answers to 1a and 1b and the correct answers for 1c:

    a. These are the titles and authors of some books on the four subjects. Many other answers are possible.

    ### *Adoption*

    United States. *Families for Black Children: The Search for Adoptive Parents.* Washington: GPO, 1971–2.

    Sorosky, Arthur, Annette Baran, and Reuben Pannor. *The Adoption Triangle.* Garden City, NY: Anchor, 1984.

    Feigelman, William and Arnold P. Silverman. *Chosen Children: New Patterns of Adoptive Relationships.* New York: Praeger, 1983.

    ### *The Internet*

    Cassidy, John. *Dot.con: The Greatest Story Ever Told.* New York: HarperCollins, 2002.

    Garfinkel, Simson. *Database Nation: The Death of Privacy in the 21st Century.* Sebastopol, CA: O'Reilly, 2000.

    Lewis, Michael. *Next: The Future Just Happened.* London: Norton, 2002.

170

Urban Violence

Anderson, Elijah. *Code of the Street: Decency, Violence, and the Moral Life of the Inner City.* London: Norton, 1999.

Decker, Scott H. et al. *Life in the Gang: Family, Friends, and Violence.* Cambridge: Cambridge UP, 1996.

Pinderhughes, Howard. *Race in the Hood: Conflict and Violence Among Urban Youth.* Minneapolis: U of Minnesota P, 1997.

Genetic Research

Cherfas, Jeremy. *Man-Made Life: An Overview of the Science, Technology, and Commerce of Genetic Engineering.* New York: Pantheon, 1982.

Kant, P. W., ed. *New Approaches to Genetics: Developments in Molecular Genetics.* Stocksfield, UK: Oriel, 1978.

Lipkin, Mack, Jr., and Peter T. Rowley, eds. *Genetic Responsibility: On Choosing Our Children's Genes.* New York: Plenum, 1974.

b. Betty Friedan's titles include *The Feminine Mystique*, *The Second Stage*, and others. John Kenneth Galbraith's titles include *The Great Crash of 1929*, *The Nature of Mass Poverty*, *The Affluent Society*, and many others.

c. *Invisible Man* was written by Ralph Ellison. (There is another book with a similar title, *The Invisible Man*, by H. G. Wells.) *A Swiftly Tilting Planet* was written by Madeleine L'Engle.

2. a. This library uses the *Library of Congress* catalog system.

b. The book's title is *The Distance Education Evolution: Issues and Case Studies*.

c. This book has three authors: Dominique Monolescu, Catherine Schifter, and Linda Greenwood.

d. The book is listed under three headings: "Distance education—Computer-assisted instruction," "Higher Education—Computer-assisted instruction," and "Educational technology."

e. The book was published in 2004.

f. No, because according to the subject listing, the book seems to focus on adult learners, especially those who take distance-learning classes. There's no indication that this book contains any information about using computers in the classroom with young children, particularly not deaf children.

3. Here is the information necessary to write a bibliography card for each title:

    a. Tuchman, Barbara. *Practicing History*. New York: Knopf, 1981.

    b. Jacobs, Lewis, ed. *The Documentary Tradition*. 2nd ed. New York: Norton, 1979.

    c. Mead, Margaret. *Coming of Age in Samoa: A Psychological Study of Primitive Youth for Western Civilization*. New York: Blue Ribbon Books, 1928.

    d. Bank, Stephen and Michael D. Kahn. *The Sibling Bond*. New York: Basic, 1982.

    e. Gross, Ronald, Beatrice Gross, and Sylvia Seidman, eds. *The New Old: Struggling for Decent Aging*. Garden City, NY: Anchor, 1978.

    f. Arnold, Matthew. *Culture and Anarchy*. Cambridge, UK: Cambridge UP, 1960.

4. The goal of this assignment is to induce students to explore various reference sources, though online ones will likely be most convenient. The answers that follow include some hints as to where the answers may be found.

    a. The Persian Gulf War began on January 17, 1991, and lasted until February 28, 1992. (Possible sources: *Facts on File*, *www.military.com*)

    b. Kodachrome film was invented by L.D. Mannes and L. Godowsky in 1935. (Possible sources: *Focal Encyclopedia of Photography*, *www. inventorsdigest.com*)

    c. *Rosacea* is a chronic disease of the skin of the face. Its symptoms include redness and pimples; it was once called *acne rosacea*. (Possible sources: *Oxford Companion to Medicine, Dorland's Illustrated Medical Dictionary*, *www. webmd.com*)

d. *Everybody Loves Raymond* was the winner of the 2003 Outstanding Comedy Series Emmy. (Possible sources: *The World Almanac*, *www.emmys.org*)

e. John Sartain was an engraver and oil painter. (Possible sources: *Dictionary of American Biography*, *National Cylopedia of American Biography*, *www.artcyclopedia.com*)

f. The first black was elected to Congress in 1868 during Reconstruction. (Possible sources: *The American Negro Reference Book*, *www.africanaonline.com*)

g. *Pareto's Law* is a law of economics that states that no matter what a nation's institutionalized economic structure the distribution of income among citizens will be the same. (Possible sources: *The Dictionary of Banking and Finance*, *The Dictionary of Business and Economics*, *The McGraw-Hill Dictionary of Modern Economics*, *www.economics.about.com*)

h. An *écorché* figure is a drawing of the human body without skin, displaying all the musculature. The word comes from the French for "flayed." Such drawings were once standard studies for art students. (Possible sources: *The Oxford Companion to Art*, *The Thames & Hudson Dictionary of Art Terms*, *www.britannica.com*)

i. The *mbira* is an African instrument played with the fingers; it is also called a *thumb piano, kalimba, marimba, sansa or sanza*, and *lamellaphone*. (Possible sources: *The New Harvard Dictionary of Music*, *Merriam-Webster Online*)

j. *Kachinas* are supernatural beings and also their masked impersonations at rituals and ceremonies. (Possible sources: *The Encyclopedia of Religion*, *American Heritage Dictionary Online*)

5. Below are some indexes, in addition to the *Reader's Guide, Social Sciences Index*, and *New York Times Index*, that might be helpful in locating periodical articles on the various topics.

a. Drug abuse in health-care professions
   Health Index
   Government Publications Index
   Nursing Abstracts

b. Ethical considerations in organ-transplant surgery
   Philosopher's Index
   Abridged Index Medicus

c. Women in prison
   Criminal Justice Abstracts
   Sociological Abstracts

d. Deforestation of the Amazon rain forest
   Environment Index
   International Political Science Abstracts

e. The difference between *Cold Mountain* as a novel and as a film
   MLA International Index, under *"Motion Picture Criticism"*
   Film Literature Index, under *"Motion Picture Review"*

6. *Answers will vary.*

7. *Answers will vary.*

8. Here are examples of possible note cards taken from paragraphs 3–8 in Robbins and Wilner's article:

174

Direct Quotation

Period of quarterlife crisis   Robbins & Wilner, p. 453

Robbins and Wilner state that the term "quarterlife" refers to "an age group that can range from late adolescence to the mid-thirties but is usually most intense in twentysomethings."

Summary

Causes of quarterlife crisis   Robbins & Wilner, pp. 453–454

The quarterlife crisis typically occurs when individuals realize that their life has lost the predictability of a stable environment, such as that of school, where goals and the means of attaining them are clear-cut. These individuals feel that they now have lost their way and are floating amid the endless array of possibilities in the "real world."

Combined note card

Contrast between midlife   Robbins & Wilner, pp. 453–454
and quarterlife crises

The most obvious difference between the crises is that the quarterlife one occurs much earlier in life than the midlife one. Another difference is that the midlife crisis is evoked when "a sense of stagnancy sparks the need for change." In contrast, the quarterlife crisis derives from a sense of anxiety about the "extreme uncertainty" about one's future after graduation. In addition, the midlife crisis is quite "widely acknowledged," while the quarterlife one is relatively unacknowledged, leaving sufferers feeling alone.

ANSWERS FOR CHAPTER 20
"WRITING THE RESEARCH PAPER"

**[Full and Brief versions only;
this chapter does not appear in the Concise Edition]**

1. Here is the correct *Works Cited* list for this paper:

    "Adolescents, TV, and Sex." *Voices in the Family.* Host Dr. Daniel Gottlieb. Prod.
     Laura Jackson. WHYY-FM, Philadelphia. 27 Sep. 2004. Radio.

    Center for Adolescent Studies at Indiana University. "Normal Adolescent
     Development." *Adolescence Directory On-Line.* 29 Sept. 1998. Web. 27 Mar.
     2002.

    López, Ralph I., M.D. "The Emotional Life of the Adolescent." *The Teen Health
     Book: A Parents' Guide to Adolescent Health and Well-Being.* New York:
     Norton, 2002. 55–70. Print.

    Parker-Pope, Tara. "Rise in Early Puberty Causes Parents to Ask, 'When Is It Too
     Soon?'" *Wall Street Journal* 21 July 2001: B1+. Print.

    Pinquart, Martin, and Rainer K. Silbereisen. "Transmission of Values from
     Adolescents to Their Parents." *Adolescence* 39.153 (2004): 83–100. Print.

    Steinberg, Laurence. "Ethnicity and Adolescent Achievement." *American Educator.*
     Summer 1996: 28–35, 44–48. Print.

    - - -. *You and Your Adolescent: A Parent's Guide for Ages 10–20.* Pennsylvania:
     HarperCollins, 1997. Print.

2. The attribution may occur at the beginning, the middle, or the end of the sentence,
    but the citation should be placed at the end. The examples below show some possible
    responses; your students will undoubtedly have different ones.

a. Journalist James Gleick argues, "If the Type A phenomenon made for poor medical research, it stands nonetheless as a triumph of social criticism. [. . .] No wonder the concept has proven too rich [. . .] to be dismissed" (450).

   "If the Type A phenomenon made for poor medical research," journalist James Gleick argues, "it stands nonetheless as a triumph of social criticism. [. . .] No wonder the concept has proven too rich [. . .] to be dismissed" (450).

   "If the Type A phenomenon made for poor medical research, it stands nonetheless as a triumph of social criticism. [. . .] No wonder the concept has proven too rich [. . .] to be dismissed," argues journalist James Gleick (450).

b. Journalist James Gleick argues that despite its failure as a scientific principle, the notion of Type A is an accurate social observation (450).

c. Here are typical sentences quoting and summarizing two of the experts that Gleick cites:

Direct Quotation

Cardiologists Meyer Friedman and Ray Rosenman offer an example of "the canonical Type A," whom they call "Paul." In describing Paul, they say, "A very disproportionate amount of his emotional energy is consumed in struggling against the normal constraints of time. 'How can I move faster, and do more and more things in less and less time?'' is the question that never ceases to torment him" (quot in Gleick 447).

Summary

Cardiologists Meyer Friedman and Ray Rosenman describe the characteristics of the typical Type A personality. The most dominant of these is a hyperconsciousness about time, resulting in an obsessive desire to get as much done as possible in the least amount of time. This concern borders on torment for the Type A personality (quot in Gleick 447).

ANSWERS FOR PART VI:
"A CONCISE HANDBOOK"

[Full version only;
Handbook does not appear in Brief Edition or Concise Edition]

Correcting Sentence Fragments (pp. 606–07)

Below are examples of how to rewrite the sentences that contain errors. Other answers, in some cases, are possible.

1. Even though there must be millions of pigeons in the city, you never see a baby pigeon. It makes you wonder where they're hiding.

2. Children between the ages of 8 and 12 often follow teenagers' trends and look up to teens as role models, mimicking their behavior in frequently disconcerting ways.

3. The least expensive remote-controlled toy car costs over 50 dollars, which is more than many budget-conscious parents want to pay. Such high costs are typical in the toy industry.

4. Correct

5. Because they feel urban schools are second-rate, many parents hope to move their families to the suburbs, even though they plan to continue working in the city.

6. Pulling the too-short hospital gown around his wasted body, the patient wandered down the hospital corridor. He was unaware of the stares of the healthy people streaming by.

7. Last year, the student government overhauled its charter and created chaos. It produced a confusing set of guidelines that muddled already contradictory policies. This year's senate has to find a way to remedy the situation.

8. Out of all the listed apartments we looked at that dreary week, only one was affordable and suitable for human habitation.

9. My grandfather likes to send offbeat greeting cards, like the one with a picture of a lion holding onto a parachute. The card reads, "Just wanted to drop you a lion."

10. About a year ago, my mother was unexpectedly laid off by the restaurant where she had been hired five years earlier as head chef. The experience made her realize that she wanted to go into business for herself.

Correcting Comma Splices and Run-On Sentences (pp. 609–10)

Below are examples of how to rewrite the sentences that contain errors. Other answers, in some cases, are possible.

1. Since the town appeared to be nearby, they left the car on the side of the road and started walking toward the village. They soon regretted their decision.

2. As we rounded the bend, we saw hundreds of crushed cars piled in neat stacks. The rusted hulks resembled flattened tin cans.

3. With unexpected intensity, the rain hit the pavement. Plumes of heat rose from the blacktop, making it difficult to drive safely.

4. According to all reports, the day after Thanksgiving is the worst day of the year to shop. The stores are jammed with people, all looking for bargains.

5. Plants should be treated regularly with an organic insecticide; otherwise, spider mites and mealybugs can destroy new growth.

6. Have you ever looked closely at a penny? Do you know whether Lincoln faces right or left?

7. As we set up the tent, flies swarmed around our heads. We felt like day-old garbage.

8. If the phone rings when my parents are eating diner, they don't answer it. They assume that, if the person wants to reach them, he or she will call back.

9. The library's security system needs improving. It allows too many people to sneak away with books and magazines hidden in their pockets, purses, or briefcases.

10. Ocean air is always bracing. It makes everyone feel relaxed and carefree, as though the world of work is far away.

Correcting Faulty Parallelism (p. 611)

1. The professor's tests were long, difficult, and anxiety producing.

2. Medical tests showed that neither a dust allergy nor seasonal hay fever caused the child's coughing fits.

3. One option that employees had was to accept a pay cut; the other was to work longer hours.

4. The hairstylist warned her customers, "I'm a beautician, not a magician. This is a comb, not a wand."

5. The renovated concert hall is both beautiful and spacious.

6. My roommates and I are learning not only Japanese but also Russian.

7. The game-show contestants were told they had to be quick-witted, friendly, and enthusiastic.

8. Correct

9. While waiting in line at the supermarket, people often flip through the tabloids to read about celebrities, the latest scandals, and weight-loss tricks.

10. Eventually, either society will make smoking illegal or people will give it up on their own.

Correcting Problems With Subject-Verb Agreement (p. 613)

1. There are many secretaries who do their bosses' jobs, as well as their own.

2. Correct

3. Each of the children wears a name tag when the playgroup takes a field trip.

4. Next week, the faculty committee on academic standards plans to pass a controversial resolution, one that the student body has rejected in the past.

5. Correct

6. Correct

7. The human spinal column, with its circular disks, resembles a stack of wobbly poker chips.

8. Both the students and the instructor dislike experimental music.

9. In most schools, either the college president or the provost is responsible for presenting the budget to the board of trustees. The board of trustees, in turn, is responsible for cutting costs whenever possible.

10. Nobody in the two classes thinks that the exam, which lasted three hours, was fair.

Correcting Problems With Verb Tense (pp. 614–15)

1. I parked illegally, so my car was towed and got dented in the process.

2. Correct

3. Although the union leaders had called a strike, the union members voted not to stop working.

4. Dr. Alice Chase wrote a number of books on healthy eating. In 1974 she died of malnutrition.

5. By the time we hiked back to the campsite, the rest of the group had collected their gear to go home.

6. Correct

7. As a boy, Thomas Edison was told he would never succeed at anything.

8. The Museum of Modern Art once hung a painting upside down. The mistake went unnoticed for more than a month.

9. When doctors in Los Angeles went on strike in 1976, the death rate dropped 18 percent.

10. John Steinbeck's *The Grapes of Wrath* conveys the horrors of poverty.

Correcting Problems With Pronoun Case (pp. 617–18)

1. At this college, neither the president nor the dean automatically assumes that, on every issue, the faculty is automatically better informed than we students.

2. Between you and me, each of the dorms should have its security system replaced.

3. The theater critic, who slipped into her seat right before the curtain went up, gave him and the other actors favorable reviews.

4. Neither of the boys impressed her or me with his musical ability.

5. The salesperson explained to my husband and me that each of the laptop computers had its drawbacks.

6. Correct

7. After enjoying prosperity through most of the 1980s, she and he were unprepared for the rigors of the next decade.

8. Correct

9. Correct

10. The people who lived next door, my roommates and I concluded, had no intention of being neighborly.

Correcting Problems With Pronoun Agreement (p. 620)

1. We proponents of the recycling plan challenged everyone on the town council to express his or her objections. Or: We proponents of the recycling plan challenged the town-council members to express their objections.

2. Correct

3. All job applicants must call for an appointment, so that the personnel office can interview them.

4. The committee passed its resolution that each of the apartments was to be free of asbestos before occupancy.

5. Typically, one of the girls loses her schedule of upcoming games, so the coach always reminds the team of its next event at the start of each competition.

6. I like living in the same small town where I was raised, because there's always someone who remembers me as a child.

7. The instructor reminded the class to pick up their term papers before leaving for semester break.

8. Correct

9. Despite poor attendance last year, the library staff decided once again to hold its annual party at the Elmhurst Inn.

10. Many amateur photographers like to use one-step cameras that they don't have to focus. Or: Many amateur photographers like to use one-step cameras that don't require focusing.

Correcting Problems With Pronoun Reference (pp. 621–22)

1. In her novels, Ann Tyler gives us a picture of family life—at its best and at its worst.

2. Lock dangerous chemicals in a storage closet to keep children away from them.

3. The student sat down glumly as soon as the professor began to criticize the student's research paper. After a few moments, though, the student turned away in frustration.

4. Many patients' lawsuits against doctors end when the patients receive out-of-court settlements.

5. All too often, arguments between a big and little sister are ended by the younger one, who threatens to blackmail her older sister with some violation of household rules.

6. In *A Doll's House*, Ibsen dramatizes the story of a woman treated as a plaything.

7. The swirling cape of the magician distracted the audience as he opened the trapdoor slowly.

8. Since the old man planned his morning around reading the newspaper, he became upset when it was delivered late.

9. The supervisor explained to the employee that the employee would be transferred soon.

10. . . . The members decided to continue the discussion the following week.

Correcting Problems With Modification (pp. 623–24)

1. While I was cooking dinner, the baby began to howl.

2. Swaying from the boughs of a tall tree, the ape displayed an agility and grace that intrigued the children.

3. When pondering her problems, Laura finally realized that her life was filled with many pleasures.

4. At the end of the semester, I realized that I needed tutoring in only one course.

5. While we were waiting for the plumber, the hot-water tank began to leak all over the basement floor.

6. Correct

7. Wandering loose, dogs and cats can scare small children.

8. With difficulty, we read the old newspaper clipping, which was faded and brittle with age.

9. The reporters indicated that they wanted only a few minutes of the candidate's time.

10. With disgust, I threw the greasy hamburger that had been dripping all over me into the trash.

Correcting Comma Errors (pp. 629–30)

1. The local movie theater, despite efforts to attract customers, finally closed its doors and was purchased by a supermarket chain.

2. Correct

3. Their parents, always risk takers, divorced in August and remarried in February, just five months later.

4. Shaken by the threat of a hostile takeover, the board of directors and the stockholders voted to sell the retail division, which had been losing money for years.

5. Despite my parents' objections, I read Stephen King's novels *The Shining* and *Carrie* when I was in junior high. The books terrified me. Nevertheless, I couldn't put them down.

6. We skimmed the chapter, looked quickly at the tables and charts, realized we didn't know enough to pass the exam, and began to panic.

7. After years of saving his money, my brother bought a used car, and then his problems started.

8. I discovered last week that my neighbors, whose friendship I had always treasured, intend to sue me.

9. Late yesterday afternoon, I realized that Dan was lying and had driven my car without permission.

10. Although it can be annoying and frustrating, forgetting things usually isn't an early sign of Alzheimer's disease, as many people think.

Correcting Problems With Punctuation (p. 640)

1. The New Madrid fault, which lies in the central part of the country, will be the site of a major earthquake within the next 30 years.

2. In the children's story, the hero carries a fresh yellow rose rather than a sword.

3. "Branch offices and drive-in windows," the bank president announced, "will be closed January 4, the day of the governor's funeral."

4. Some people avoid physical work. Others seek out and enjoy it, but probably no one likes it all the time.

5. The scientists said that they wondered how anyone could believe stories of outer-space visitors.

6. On the office's paneled walls, the executive had a framed copy of the poem "If."

7. Correct

8. Shoplifters often believe they are doing no harm; nevertheless, shoplifting is stealing and, therefore, illegal.

9. The young people fell in love with the house that stood next to a clear, cold stream.

10. The kennel owner sent birthday cards and small gifts to all the dogs she had boarded during the year.

Correcting Problems With Mechanics and Spelling (p. 648)

1. *Emerging Nations in Today's World*, one of the supplementary texts in Modern History I, is on reserve at the library.

2. Last year, while visiting my parents in central Florida, I took a disastrous course in sociology.

3. The analysts of the election-eve poll concluded, "It's a toss-up."

4. For some reason, spring tends to have a depressing effect on me.

5. Reverend Astor's teeth chattered at my brother's outdoor wedding, held in March in northern Massachusetts.

6. Weighing in at 122 pounds was Tim Fox, a sophomore from a community college in Alabama.

7. In the fall, when the foliage is at its peak, many people pack their hiking gear and head for the country.

8. Three hundred students signed up for the experimental seminar that Prof. Julia Cruz plans to offer through the Business Department. The class is scheduled to meet at 8 a.m. on Monday.

9. Senator Miller, who was supposed to end the press conference once the subject of the environment came up, got embroiled in an argument with several reporters.

10. Listen to nutritionists; many of them contend that there are advantages to limiting the amount of protein in your diet.